航空服务艺术与管理本科系列教材

客舱播音艺术
In-flight Announcement

王建惠　刘　超◎主　编
黄　晨◎副主编

电子工业出版社
Publishing House of Electronics Industry
北京·BEIJING

未经许可，不得以任何方式复制或抄袭本书之部分或全部内容。
版权所有，侵权必究。

图书在版编目（CIP）数据

客舱播音艺术 / 王建惠，刘超主编. —北京：电子工业出版社，2024.1
ISBN 978-7-121-46712-7

Ⅰ. ①客… Ⅱ. ①王… ②刘… Ⅲ. ①民用航空－乘务人员－商业服务－播音－语言艺术－教材
Ⅳ. ①F560.9

中国国家版本馆 CIP 数据核字（2023）第 221697 号

责任编辑：刘淑丽
印　　刷：中煤（北京）印务有限公司
装　　订：中煤（北京）印务有限公司
出版发行：电子工业出版社
　　　　　北京市海淀区万寿路 173 信箱　邮编：100036
开　　本：787×1 092　1/16　印张：11.75　字数：311 千字
版　　次：2024 年 1 月第 1 版
印　　次：2024 年 10 月第 2 次印刷
定　　价：48.00 元

凡所购买电子工业出版社图书有缺损问题，请向购买书店调换。若书店售缺，请与本社发行部联系，联系及邮购电话：(010) 88254888，88258888。
质量投诉请发邮件至 zlts@phei.com.cn，盗版侵权举报请发邮件至 dbqq@phei.com.cn。
本书咨询联系方式：(010) 88254182，liusl@phei.com.cn。

航空服务艺术与管理本科系列教材建设委员会

丛书总主编：

刘　永　　北京中航未来科技集团有限公司董事长

丛书总策划：

王益友　　中国东方航空集团驻国外办事处原经理，教授

丛书编委会秘书长：

胡明良　　江南影视艺术职业学院航空乘务学院副院长

丛书编委会成员：（按姓氏笔画数排序，姓氏笔画数相同者，按姓名第 2 个字笔画数排序）

刘岩松　　沈阳航空航天大学民用航空学院院长

刘　超　　华侨大学厦航学院副院长兼空乘系主任

李广春　　郑州航空工业管理学院民航学院院长

张树生　　山东交通学院航空学院原院长、山东通用航空研究院院长

陈　健　　北华航天工业学院外国语学院院长

郑步生　　南京航空航天大学金城学院航空运输与工程学院院长

宫新军　　滨州学院乘务学院院长

熊越强　　桂林航天工业学院教授

前　　言

随着中国民航业的蓬勃发展，民航业的国际化程度日益提高。航空公司对空乘人员的英语水平和职业素养提出了较高的要求。客舱广播是乘务员客舱服务工作流程中的重要环节。正确、规范地朗读广播词对航班顺利和安全执飞起到至关重要的作用。本教材是编者们在总结多年课堂教学经验的基础上同拥有企业客舱服务工作经历的一线教师共同编写的。本教材有利于学生在模拟实际工作的情景中，练习并掌握原汁原味的客舱服务英语。本教材基于任务驱动的项目化教学方式，通过对所学知识点及技能点的分析、梳理，选取了包含介绍登机广播、安全演示、客舱安全检查、餐食广播、应急处置广播、落地后返航广播、送别广播等32项主要职业活动作为任务。每个任务包括问题导入、背景知识、朗读训练、词汇和短语、技巧点拨、实战练习6个部分。

本教材凸显"客舱广播"的专业性，以"实用为主、够用为度、应用为目的"为原则，契合实际工作岗位所需的专业知识和英语技能，围绕工作情境设计与实训任务，培养学生以"听、说、练"为主的语言交际技能，构建学生的语言知识技能和职业能力体系。每个项目以工作任务为驱动，围绕工作任务来编排内容，注重培养学生综合应用能力及创新解决问题的能力。本教材内容翔实、语言精练，集功能性、知识性和实用性于一体，是一本极具特色的民航专业英语学习用教材。

本教材由陕西职业技术学院旅游与文化学院王建惠老师、华侨大学空乘学院刘超老师、天津交通职业学院黄晨老师、西北航空训练股份有限公司培训部负责人武贤伟共同编写。本教材提供了完整的配套教学资料，包括电子课件和在线课程音、视频资料，在每个任务的最后均配有习题，读者可以通过这些习题对所学知识进行巩固、加深理解，并学会运用所学知识解决实际问题。本教材在附录部分增加了词汇和表达，便于读者查阅。

本教材可作为航空服务艺术与管理专业、空中乘务专业本（专）科学生的教学用书，也可以作为民航企业及各培训机构的空乘人员岗前培训教材，还可作为具有一定英语基础的旅客自学用书。本教材在编写过程中参考了近年来民航乘务方面的相关书籍及文献资料，在此对相关人员表示诚挚的谢意。由于编者水平有限，教材中难免有疏漏或不妥之处，恳请专家及读者不吝指正。

2023年7月

目 录

Task 1　Check-in and Departure ……………………………………………… 1

Task 2　Notice of Flight Cancellation ………………………………………… 7

Task 3　Flight Delay Announcement ………………………………………… 13

Task 4　Baggage Arrangement ………………………………………………… 18

Task 5　Boarding ………………………………………………………………… 23

Task 6　Welcome Speech ……………………………………………………… 27

Task 7　Flight Route Introduction …………………………………………… 32

Task 8　Safety Check Broadcast ……………………………………………… 37

Task 9　Emergency Exit ………………………………………………………… 42

Task 10　Fasten the Seat Belt ………………………………………………… 47

Task 11　Safety Demonstration ……………………………………………… 52

Task 12　Life Vest ……………………………………………………………… 57

Task 13　Smoking Prohibition ………………………………………………… 63

Task 14　Restrictions on Electronic Devices ……………………………… 69

Task 15　Transfer Flight Information ……………………………………… 74

Task 16　Stopover Flight Reminder ………………………………………… 79

Task 17　Level Flight …………………………………………………………… 84

Task 18　Declaration Card …………………………………………………… 90

Task 19　Shopping ……………………………………………………………… 95

Task 20　Meals ………………………………………………………………… 101

Task 21　Beverages …………………………………………………………… 106

Task 22　Ground Temperature ……………………………………………… 111

Task 23　Recreation …………………………………………………………… 116

Task 24　Turbulence …………………………………………………………… 121

Task 25　Air Traffic Control ………………………………………………… 126

Task 26	On Stopover	132
Task 27	Air Condition Problem	138
Task 28	Safety Check Broadcast before Landing	144
Task 29	Landing on the Ground	149
Task 30	Returning to the Departure Airport	154
Task 31	Landing at the Destination Airport	159
Task 32	Seeing off	164
Appendix	Words and Expressions	169

Task 1
Check-in and Departure

Respect guests.

尊重客人。

微课抢先看

Learning Objectives
Knowledge Objectives 1. To learn some useful words and expressions 2. To conduct an announcement related to subject **Skill Objectives** 1. To be able to master reading skill of classification of the cabin broadcast 2. To be able to perform at the workplace effectively and rightly **Quality Objectives** 1. To develop the sense of responsibility 2. To be knowledgeable and professional

Part I Lead-in

Question:

(1) Have you ever heard of any announcements at the airport?

(2) What time should the passengers get to the airport?

Part II Background Information

值机：为旅客办理乘机手续（换登机牌，安排座位，托运行李等）。以前机场由武警值守，登机前验明身份，所以国内叫"值机"，英文名为 check in。国内航线最迟值机时间一般为起飞前 40 分钟或 45 分钟，国际航线为 60 分钟。

Part III Let's Read

1. Passengers taking Flight No.9947 to Beijing, attention please. Please go to the counter No. 37 to exchange your boarding passes for transit passes. Thank you.

搭乘 9947 航班飞往北京的乘客，请注意。请前往 37 号柜台，将您的登机牌换成过境证。谢谢。

2. Ladies and gentlemen, may I have your attention please? Standby passengers for Flight No.1754 to Hangzhou, please go to the counter No. 25 for check-in.

女士们，先生们：

请注意。前往杭州的 1754 号航班的候补乘客，请前往 25 号柜台办理登机手续。

Task 1 Check-in and Departure

3. Ladies and gentlemen, Flight CA1234 to Tianjin is now ready for check-in. Passengers on this flight, please have your belongings ready and proceed to the counter No. 12. Thank you.

女士们，先生们：

飞往天津的 CA1234 次航班，现在开始办理登机手续。请乘坐此次航班的旅客，拿好随身物品，到 12 号柜台办理。谢谢！

4. Ladies and gentlemen, attention, please. The check-in counter for Flight CA1234 bound for Tianjin will be closed in 30 minutes. Passengers who have not gone through check-in formalities, please go to the check-in counter as soon as possible. Thank you for your cooperation.

女士们，先生们：

请注意。飞往天津的 CA1234 次航班，即将在 30 分钟后办完登机手续。还未办理登机手续的旅客，请尽快到值机柜台办理。感谢您的配合！

5. Ladies and gentlemen, may I have your attention, please? Flight CA1234 will take off in 20 minutes. All passengers for this flight please go to the gate No. 12 and board the aircraft immediately.

Thank you.

女士们，先生们：

请注意。CA1234 次航班将在 20 分钟后起飞。请乘坐本次航班的旅客，马上到 12 号登机口登机。谢谢！

Part IV Words and Expressions

1. announce /əˈnaʊns/ vt. 宣布；预示；播报

    announcement n. 通知，公告

    make an announcement 发布通知

    cabin announcement 客舱广播

2. ready /ˈredi/ adj. 准备好的；现成的

    to be ready for（prepared for）为……做好准备

    to get ready for 为……做准备（强调准备的动作）

3. passenger /ˈpæsɪndʒə(r)/ n. 旅客；乘客

4. check in 到达并登记；报到

5. proceed to 去往（某地）

6. due to (because of) ……的原因

7. delay / dɪˈleɪ/ *v.* 推迟；延误

Part V Reading Skill

客舱广播词的分类

Classification of the Cabin Broadcast

客舱广播词，可以分为：

（1）问候类，包括欢迎词、节日、致意、着陆；

（2）信息告知类，包括航班信息、注意事项、检疫入境规定；

（3）解释类，包括误机、返航、取消航班、备降；

（4）紧急情况类，包括代机长广播、迫降。

想要在客舱广播时表现得出色，就必须了解每种类型广播词的特点，用相应的情感进行广播，这是航空播音的一个技巧。像问候类的广播词，在情感上要亲切、真诚，声音要柔和甜美，语速要舒缓。信息告知类的广播词事先必须做好充分的准备，信息要准确，语言清晰，重点突出，语速适中。解释类的广播词则要广播及时，信息准确，语气诚恳，语速适中。对于紧急情况类的广播词，则要有权威性、要冷静，语气坚定干练，信息准确，声音洪亮，语速可稍快。掌握这些广播词的特点，有助于我们更好地把握自己的情感，在广播时更人性化、更细致化。

Part VI Practical Practice

1. Match the expressions in Column A with their Chinese equivalents in Column B.

Column A	Column B
(1) bound for	a. 通过
(2) formality	b. 值机柜台
(3) proceed	c. 柜台
(4) check-in counter	d. 立即，马上
(5) go through	e. 合作
(6) cooperation	f. 随身物品，所有物
(7) immediately	g. 开始行动，继续做
(8) belongings	h. 飞往……
(9) counter	i. 旅客
(10) passenger	j. 正式手续

Task 1 Check-in and Departure

2. Translate the following sentences into English.

（1）请乘坐此次航班的旅客，拿好随身物品，到1号柜台办理值机。

（2）还未办理登机手续的旅客，请尽快到值机柜台办理。

（3）CA1234次航班将在30分钟后起飞。

（4）飞往上海的CA1234次航班，即将在20分钟后办完登机手续。

3. Translate the following sentences into Chinese.

(1) Passengers for this flight, please board through the gate No.12.

(2) We hope you will enjoy your flight.

(3) We apologize for the inconvenience.

(4) May I have your attention, please?

4. Practice oral English.

(1) Thank you for waiting. Ladies and gentlemen,

Flight _____ for _____ is now ready for boarding. Will passengers on this flight please make their way to the gate _____. Please refrain from smoking beyond the gate.

Thank you.

(2) Attention please.

This is the final call for passengers traveling to _____. _____ is now boarding. Passengers are kindly requested to proceed to the gate _____.

Thank you.

(3) Ladies and gentlemen,

May I have your attention, please? Check-in counters for Flight _____ bound for _____ will be closed in half an hour. Passengers who have not done check-in formalities, please go to the check-in counters immediately.

We hope you will enjoy your flight with_____(airlines).

Thank you.

(4) Ladies and gentlemen,

May I have your attention, please? The gate number for Flight _____ has changed from ___ to ___. Passengers for this flight please board through the gate No. ____. We apologize for the inconvenience.

Thank you.

(5) Attention please.

_____(airlines) announces the departure of Flight_____ to _____. Will passengers for this flight please proceed to the gate_____?

Thank you.

(6) Ladies and gentlemen,

May I have your attention, please? Flight _____ will be departing in ___ minutes. All passengers for this flight, please make your way to the gate No. ____. We wish you a good flight.

Thank you.

Task 2
Notice of Flight Cancellation

微课抢先看

Guests first, service first.
宾客至上，服务第一。

Learning Objectives
Knowledge Objectives 1. To make the notice of flight cancellation 2. To learn some useful expressions about notice of flight cancellation **Skill Objectives** 1. To be able to master the words and expressions 2. To be able to get to use the correct broadcast speed **Quality Objectives** 1. To develop the sense of responsibility 2. To be knowledgeable and professional

Part I Lead-in

Question:

Dialogue

A: I'm here for Flight 513 to New York, but I thought I heard the paging system announce that it is canceled. Is that true?

B: I'm terribly sorry, sir, but I'm afraid it is true. That flight has been canceled. Would you like to try to book tomorrow's flight?

Do you know how to announce a notice of Flight Cancellation?

Part II　Background Information

航班取消：由于机务维护、航班调配、商务、机组等原因，造成航班延误或取消，航空公司将向旅客提供航班动态信息、安排餐食或住宿等服务。由于天气、突发事件、空中交通管制、安检以及旅客等非承运人原因，造成航班延误或取消，机场方面可向旅客提供航班动态信息，协助旅客安排餐食和住宿，费用由旅客自理。

Part III　Let's Read

1. Ladies and gentlemen, may I have your attention please?

We regret to announce that Flight CA5128 from Guiyang has been canceled due to

① the poor weather condition at our airport;

② the poor weather condition over the air route;

③ the poor weather condition at Guiyang airport;

④ aircraft reallocation;

⑤ the maintenance of the aircraft;

⑥ the aircraft maintenance at Guiyang airport;

⑦ air traffic congestion;

⑧ the close-down of Guiyang airport;

Task 2 Notice of Flight Cancellation

⑨ communication trouble.

(This flight has been rescheduled to tomorrow at 13:40.)

Thank you.

女士们，先生们，请注意。

我们抱歉地通知，由贵阳飞来的CA5128次航班由于

① 本机场天气不够飞行标准；

② 航路天气不够飞行标准；

③ 贵阳机场天气不够飞行标准；

④ 飞机调配原因；

⑤ 飞机机械原因；

⑥ 飞机在贵阳机场出现机械故障；

⑦ 航行管制原因；

⑧ 贵阳机场关闭；

⑨ 通信原因。

（本航班将改期至明日13时40分到达。）

谢谢！

2. Passengers of CA1234 to Tianjin. Attention please. I'm sorry to tell you that your flight has been canceled because of _____. We sincerely apologize for this inconvenience caused.

前往天津的旅客请注意，我们抱歉地通知，您乘坐的CA1234次航班，由于_____原因，决定取消今日飞行，对于带给您的不便，我们深表歉意。

Part IV Words and Expressions

1. cancel /ˈkænsl/ *v.* 删去，划掉；取消

2. reallocation /ˌriːˌæləˈkeɪʃn/ *n.* 再分配

   aircraft reallocation 飞机调配

3. maintain /meɪnˈteɪn/ *v.* 保持，维持

   the maintenance of the aircraft 因飞机机械故障而进行维护

   maintain a highway 保养公路

   maintain one's family 供养家庭

   maintenance *n.* 保持，维持

4. congestion /kənˈdʒestʃən/ *n.* 拥挤；堵塞
   air traffic congestion 空中交通堵塞

Part V　Reading Skill

使用正确的广播语速
Use the Correct Reading Speed

语速是指朗读时的快慢程度。慢读与快读都有一定标准。慢读，重在读准词、词组、短语、意群和句子的基础上，注意语言速度。慢中求准，慢中求快。因此，慢读的速度应该根据自己的实际情况而定。快读，即以每分钟148个音节左右的正常语速朗读，或根据内容上的需要朗读。语速影响听的效果，所以语速不可太快或太慢，否则达不到"让人听清楚"的目的。语速过快会造成句子重音、意群和节奏方面的错误，还会造成发音不到位、加音、吞音、误读以及移行时的突然中断，影响意思的表达。要力求读准，发音清楚、正确。当然，朗读并不是越慢越好。随着熟练程度的提高和朗读技巧的掌握，语速可以逐步加快。朗读应力求流利。正常情况下的客舱广播无论中文或英文，应注意放慢语速、放缓语气。我们可以将自己的广播进行录音回放，并换位思考：第一次乘坐飞机的旅客能否听清我们播报的内容并且有记忆的时间呢？理想的播音速度是每分钟240~250个字符，这符合人耳对熟悉语言的接受和辨析度。

Part VI　Practical Practice

1. Match the expressions in Column A with their Chinese equivalents in Column B.

Column A　　　　　　　　　　　Column B

(1) attention　　　　　　　　　　a. 由于；应归于

(2) reallocation　　　　　　　　　b. 再分配

(3) maintain　　　　　　　　　　c. 取消

(4) inconvenience　　　　　　　　d. 航班

(5) due to　　　　　　　　　　　e. 道歉

(6) apologize　　　　　　　　　　f. 延误

(7) cancel　　　　　　　　　　　g. 拥挤

(8) congestion　　　　　　　　　h. 不便

(9) flight　　　　　　　　　　　i. 保养，维护

(10) delay　　　　　　　　　　　j. 注意

Task 2 Notice of Flight Cancellation

2. Translate the following sentences into English.

（1）感谢您的合作。

（2）我们抱歉地通知您，由于天气原因，已取消今日飞行。

（3）对于给各位带来的不便，我们深表歉意。

3. Translate the following sentences into Chinese.

(1) Flight CA1234 to Shanghai has been canceled because of weather conditions at local airport.

(2) We regret to announce that Flight CA1234 from Guiyang has been canceled due to air traffic congestion.

(3) This flight has been rescheduled to tomorrow at 13:40.

4. Practice oral English.

(1) Attention please.

_____ (airlines) Flight _____ to _____ has been canceled because of weather conditions at local airport. Will passengers please collect your hand baggage and go to the rear exit of this lounge. Please have your passports ready and proceed downstairs to counter _____ where information about booking, refund and alternative transport is available.

(2) Attention please.

_____ (airlines) Flight _____ to _____ will be delayed because of weather conditions at _____ Airport. A further announcement will be made not later than _____ (time). In the meantime, passengers are invited to take light refreshments with the compliments of the airlines at the buffet in this lounge.

(3) Ladies and gentlemen,

Please remain seated while we are waiting for (some passengers/ transit passengers) to get on board.

Thank you for your understanding!

(4) Ladies and gentlemen,

As more food will be sent to the aircraft for the occasion, there will be a short delay for a few minutes.

Thank you for your understanding!

(5) Ladies and gentlemen,

As the loading documents have not been sent to the aircraft, there will be a delay for a few minutes.

Thank you for your understanding!

(6) Ladies and gentlemen,

I'm sorry to have to inform you that operational requirements have made it necessary for us to transfer to another aircraft. Please disembark with all your personal effects and follow our ground staff to the new aircraft. We apologize for the inconvenience.

Thank you for your cooperation!

Task 3
Flight Delay Announcement

微课抢先看

God helps those who help themselves.
天助自助者。

Learning Objectives
Knowledge Objectives
1. To learn some useful words and expressions
2. To conduct an announcement related to subject
Skill Objectives
1. To be able to identify levels of core skills and perform at the workplace
2. To be able to apply core skill of four major factors of cabin broadcasting
Quality Objectives
1. To develop the sense of responsibility
2. To be knowledgeable and professional

Part I Lead-in

Question:

(1) Do you know how to announce flight delay?

(2) Have you ever heard of the delay announcements at the airport?

Part II　Background Information

There are many types of delays.
航班延误的类型有很多种。

1. Weather Reasons　天气原因
2. Air Traffic Control 空中管制
3. Airport Reasons 机场原因
5. Passenger Reasons 旅客原因
4. Airlines Reasons 航空公司原因

Part III　Let's Read

1. Ladies and gentlemen,

I'm sorry to inform you that we have to wait another 15 minutes for take-off because of the runway is occupied.

Thank you.

女士们，先生们，非常抱歉地通知大家，由于跑道占用原因，我们再过 15 分钟才能起飞。谢谢。

2. Ladies and gentlemen,

I'm sorry to have to inform you that operational requirements have made it necessary for us to transfer to another aircraft. Please disembark with all your personal effects and follow our ground staff to the new aircraft. We apologize for the inconvenience.

Thank you for your cooperation.

女士们，先生们，非常抱歉地通知大家，由于机械故障，我们需要换乘另一架飞机。请您带好您的个人物品下飞机，随同地面值班人员去搭乘另一架飞机。对于给各位带来的不便，我们深表歉意。

感谢大家的合作。

3. Ladies and gentlemen,

May I have your attention please? China Eastern Airlines Flight MU8667 to Shanghai will be delayed because of weather conditions at Tianjin Binhai International Airport. A further announcement will be made not later than 10:30. In the meantime passengers are invited to take light refreshments with the compliments of the airlines at the buffet in this lounge.

女士们，先生们，请注意。由于天津滨海国际机场上空天气原因，飞往上海的东航 MU8667 次航班将延误起飞，起飞时间请听 10:30 之前的广播，现在请乘客们到候机室餐饮部免费享用航空公司提供的点心。

4. Ladies and gentlemen,

Sichuan Airlines regrets to announce the delay in the departure of Flight 3U2342 to Beijing. Due to technical reasons, this flight is now expected to depart at 13:40 local time.

女士们，先生们，四川航空公司很抱歉地通知各位，前往北京的川航 3U2342 次航班，将延误起飞。由于技术上的原因，预计该航班于当地时间 13:40 起飞。

Part IV   Words and Expressions

1. delay /dɪˈleɪ/ v. 延误，延迟；延期；推迟

2. occupied /ˈɒkjupaɪd/ adj. 使用中；忙于；被侵占的

3. operational /ˌɒpəˈreɪʃ(ə)l/ adj. 操作的；运转的；运营的；业务的

4. requirement /rɪˈkwaɪəmənt/ n. 要求；必要条件

5. transfer /trænsˈfɜː(r)/ v. （使）转移；搬迁
6. cooperation /kəʊˌɒpəˈreɪʃ(ə)n/ n. 合作，协作
7. refreshments /rɪˈfreʃmənts/ n. 饮料，点心，茶点
8. compliment /ˈkɒmplɪmənt/ n. 赞扬，称赞
9. buffet /ˈbʌfeɪ/ n. 自助餐；饮食柜台；（车站）快餐部
10. lounge /laʊndʒ/ n. （机场等的）等候室，候机厅
    the departure lounge 候机室

Part V　Reading Skill

客舱广播的四大主要因素
Four Major Factors of Cabin Broadcasting

客舱广播是指在服务过程中，空乘人员借助一定的词汇、语气、语调、身体语言表达思想、感情、意愿，与旅客进行交流的一种沟通方式。客舱广播是直接影响客舱服务质量的重要因素，所以高品质的客舱广播能提升我们的服务品质。

1. 标准的中英文发音

标准的发音是广播的基础，完成一次好的广播需要我们掌握流利的中英文，因此我们平时需要多听，多读，多练，从而培养自己的发音和语感。

2. 不同时间段的广播语调

不同时间段的广播语气应做适当调整，例如，夜航应适当降低音量，下降致意语气应表现出热情，欢快并且适当升高音量等。

3. 适当的语速

我们一定要放慢自己的语调和语速，让旅客既能听得清晰也能感受到亲切。

4. 标准的坐姿

良好的坐姿能让我们拥有饱满的气息去读好每一次客舱广播，所以广播时端正自己的坐姿能让我们事半功倍。

Part VI　Practical Practice

1. Match the expressions in Column A with their Chinese equivalents in Column B.

　　Column A　　　　　　　　Column B
　　(1) delay　　　　　　　　a. 转移

(2) transfer   b. 候机厅

(3) refreshments   c. 合作

(4) lounge   d. 点心

(5) cooperation   e. 延误

2. Translate the following sentences into English.

（1）起飞时间请听 10:30 之前的广播。

（2）由于天津滨海国际机场上的天气原因，飞往上海的东航 MU8667 次航班将延误起飞。

3. Translate the following sentences into Chinese.

(1) I'm sorry to inform you that we have to wait another 15 minutes for take-off because of the runway is occupied.

(2) Please disembark with all your personal effects and follow our ground staff to the new aircraft.

4. Practice oral English.

(1) Ladies and gentlemen,

We sincerely apologize for the delay due to___ (unfavorable weather conditions/ aircraft late arrival/ air traffic control/ airport congestion/ mechanical problems/ waiting for some passengers).

Together with my team, we will try our best to make the rest of your journey as pleasant and comfortable as possible.

We thank you for your patience and understanding.

(2) Ladies and gentlemen,

We are still waiting for the boarding bridge (shuttle bus/ ramp). Please remain seated, and we will inform you to disembark as soon as the air bridge arrives.

Thank you for your understanding.

Task 4

Baggage Arrangement

微课抢先看

Service-oriented, excellence, customer first, and common development.
服务为本、精益求精、乘客为先、共同发展。

Learning Objectives
Knowledge Objectives 1. To learn some useful expressions about arranging baggage 2. To conduct an announcement related to subject **Skill Objectives** 1. To be able to know the reading skill of intonation—rising tone 2. To be able to perform at the workplace effectively and rightly **Quality Objectives** 1. To develop the serious work attitude and the sense of responsibility 2. To be knowledgeable and professional

Part I Lead-in

Question:

(1) Where can passengers know the seat number?

(2) If you can't find your seat, how can you do?

(3) How to help passengers arrange their baggage in the cabin?

(4) How to arrange seats for passengers in the cabin?

Task 4　Baggage Arrangement

Part II　Background Information

我国各个航空公司的原则是，只要是同等位，座位先到先坐。无论票价是多少元，只要舱位相同，乘客购买机票后，可登录对应航空公司的网站进行网上值机并选择座位，亦可到达机场后到相应的人工值机柜台或自助值机柜台办理登机手续，选择座位。座位选定后，不可随意调换座位。对于乘务员而言，应注意机上座位安排的一般原则：

（1）请乘客对号入座。
（2）沟通机组预留座。
（3）在符合飞机载重平衡要求的前提下，乘务员要尽量满足乘客提出的要求，安排座位。
（4）重要乘客安排在预留的最前排座位，或按照乘客意愿安排座位。
（5）对于需特殊照顾的乘客，安排在靠近乘务员的座位或者靠近窗口座位就座。
（6）身材高大的乘客应安排在宽处。

Part III　Let's Read

1. Ladies and gentlemen,

We must keep the balance of the aircraft, so please take your seat according to your seat number.

Thank you for your cooperation!

女士们，先生们，为了保持飞机的平衡，请根据您的座位号入座。感谢您的合作！

2. Ladies and gentlemen,

Welcome aboard Tianjin Airlines. Please take your seat according to your seat number. Your seat number is on the edge of the rack. Please make sure your hand baggage is stored in the overhead locker. Any small articles can be put under the seat in front of you. Please take your seat as soon as possible to keep the aisle clear for others to go through.

Thank you!

女士们，先生们：

欢迎您搭乘天津航空公司的班机旅行，请您根据登机牌上的号码对号入座，座位号码位于行李架边缘。确保您的手提行李放在行李架上，小件物品放在您前排座椅下方。请您尽快入座，以保持过道畅通，方便其他旅客顺利通过。谢谢！

Part IV Words and Expressions

1. balance /ˈbæləns/ *n.* 均衡；平衡
2. cooperation /kəʊˌɒpəˈreɪʃ(ə)ʌ/ *n.* 合作，协作；协助
3. welcome /ˈwelkəm/ *v.* 欢迎，迎接；欣然接受 *adj.* 受欢迎的；令人愉快的
   welcome aboard 欢迎登机
4. edge /edʒ/ *n.* 边缘
5. baggage /ˈbæɡɪdʒ/ *n.* 行李；偏见，（luggage）行李
6. overhead /ˌəʊvəˈhed, ˈəʊvəhed/ *adj.* 上面的；高架的；头顶上的
   overhead locker 行李架

Part V Reading Skill

升调
Intonation—Rising Tone

升调：升调多用来表示"不肯定"和"未完结"的意思，比如：
一般疑问句，语气婉转的祈使句以及用陈述句子形式表示疑问的各类句子。例如：

(1) Shall I tell him to come and see you?（一般疑问句的正常语调。）

(2) You like him?（用于陈述句形式的疑问句中，期待得到对方证实。）

(3) What have you got there?（用于特殊疑问句中，语气亲切热情。）

(4) Right you are. （用于某些感叹句中，表示轻快、活泼、鼓励等意义。）

(5) She bought red, yellow and green rugs. （用于排比句中，区别语义。）

Part VI   Practical Practice

1. Match the expressions in Column A with their Chinese equivalents in Column B.

Column A   Column B
(1) article   a. 边缘
(2) edge   b. 行李
(3) baggage   c. 物品
(4) locker   d. 储物柜
(5) aisle   e. 过道

2. Translate the following sentences into English.

（1）座位号码位于行李架边缘。

（2）小件物品建议您放在您前排座椅的下方。

3. Translate the following sentences into Chinese.

(1) Please take your seat according to your seat number.

(2) Please take your seat as soon as possible to keep the aisle clear for others to go through.

4. Practice oral English.

Ladies and gentlemen,

Welcome aboard flight CA1234 from Tianjin to Guangzhou. Would you please check your ticket and boarding pass again to make sure you're boarding the right flight?

As you enter the cabin, we kindly ask you that take your seat as soon as possible to give room for other passengers who may be standing in the aisle behind you.

Your seat number is indicated on the bottom edge of the overhead baggage compartment. Please place your carry-on baggage in the overhead compartment.

Small or fragile baggage should be placed under the seat in front of you.

Please do not leave any baggage either in the aisle or near an exit door.

Thank you for your cooperation!

Task 5 Boarding

Our services will surely satisfy all your needs.
我们的服务绝对让您满意。

微课抢先看

Learning Objectives

Knowledge Objectives

1. To know how to make an announcement of boarding

2. To learn some useful expressions about boarding

Skill Objectives

1. To be able to master the key words and expressions on board

2. To be able to get to know how to use intonation—falling tone

Quality Objectives

1. To familiarize with the workflow of boarding and develop the sense of responsibility

2. To be knowledgeable and professional

Part I Lead-in

Question:

How to greet the passengers when they are boarding?

Part II Background Information

在乘客开始登机时，客舱乘务员在客舱内指定区域就位，面带微笑，迎接乘客的到来。有时候，乘务长也可以指定乘务员到其他地点迎客，例如登机桥末端。当遇到年老或带小孩的乘客时，乘务员会主动为他们提供帮助，以保证整个登机过程顺利快速地进行。乘务员查看乘客的登机牌后，向其指引正确的方向，帮助乘客尽快找到座位。除了问候乘客外，机组成员还将播放广播欢迎词。

Part III Let's Read

1. Good morning (afternoon, evening), ladies and gentlemen,

Welcome aboard Air China Flight CA1234, from Tianjin to Guangzhou. Our plane will be taking off immediately, please fasten your seat belt, and make sure your seat back is straight up, your tray table is closed. The purser with all cabin crew members will be sincerely at your service. We hope you enjoy the flight! Thank you!

女士们，先生们，早上（下午、晚上）好。

欢迎乘坐中国国际航空公司从天津飞往广州的CA1234航班。我们的飞机马上要起飞了，请您系好安全带，收起座椅靠背，收起小桌板。乘务长和全体机组人员竭诚为您服务。希望您旅途愉快！谢谢！

2. Good morning (afternoon, evening), ladies and gentlemen,

Welcome aboard Tianjin Airlines Flight CA1234 from Tianjin to Guangzhou. We are flying to Guangzhou, the whole flight takes about 3 hours and 15 minutes, would you please check your ticket and boarding pass again to make sure you're boarding the correct flight. Thank you!

女士们，先生们，早上（下午、晚上）好。

欢迎您乘坐天津航空 CA1234 次航班由天津前往广州，由天津至广州的空中飞行时间大约为 3 小时 15 分钟。请各位旅客确认机票与登机牌以免误乘航班。谢谢!

Part IV   Words and Expressions

1. cabin /ˈkæbɪn/ n. 小木屋；机舱

   Cabin Crew（CA）乘务员，乘务长，空中乘务员

   Flight Attendant（复数：Flight Attendants） 空中乘务员

   Air Hostess（复数：Air Hostesses） 女乘务员

   Stewardess（复数：Stewardesses） 男乘务员

2. seat number 座位号

3. boarding card/pass 登机牌

4. fasten /ˈfɑːsn/ v. 系牢；钉牢；使坚固或稳固

   fasten your seatbelt 系好安全带

5. seatbelt /ˈsiːtbelt/ n. 安全带

Part V   Reading Skill

降调
Intonation—Falling Tone

降调：降调表示"肯定"和"完结"。一般用于陈述句、特殊疑问句、命令句和感叹句中。例如：

(1) Swimming is my favorite∈sport. （用于陈述句表示肯定的意义。）

(2) What did you find∈there? （用于特殊疑问句表示说话人浓厚的兴趣。）

(3) Tell me all about∈it. （用于语气较强的命令。）

(4) Have you got the∈tickets? （用于一般疑问句表示说话人的态度粗率、不耐烦或不高兴。）

(5) How∈nice! （用于感叹句，表示感叹。）

英语中除了升调、降调这两种最基本的语调外，还有降—升调、升—降调、升—降—升调、平调等。我们掌握了基本的升降调后，可以大量阅读以增加语感。

Part VI Practical Practice

1. Match the expressions in Column A with their Chinese equivalents in Column B.

Column A   Column B

(1) stewardess   a. 正确的

(2) seatbelt   b. 乘务员

(3) flight   c. 安全带

(4) check   d. 检查

(5) correct   e. 航班

2. Translate the following sentences into English.

（1）欢迎乘坐中国国际航空公司从天津飞往广州的 CA1234 航班。

（2）希望您旅途愉快。

3. Translate the following sentences into Chinese.

(1) Would you please check your ticket and boarding pass again to make sure you're boarding the correct flight?

(2) The purser Cindy with all cabin crew members will be sincerely at your service.

4. Practice oral English.

Ladies and gentlemen,

Now the plane will be taking off and the flight attendants will do safety check. Please fasten your seatbelts, stow your tray table, return your footrest to its initial position and put your seat back to the upright position. Please help us by opening the sunshades. Your cooperation will be appreciated.

Thank you.

Task 6

Welcome Speech

微课抢先看

Nothing is difficult to the man who will try.
世上无难事，只要肯登攀。

Learning Objectives
Knowledge Objectives 1.To know how to make an announcement of welcome speech 2. To learn some useful expressions about speech of welcome **Skill Objectives** 1. To be able to use the key words and the expressions 2. To be able to get to know the voice turbidity **Quality Objectives** 1. To cultivate a sense of service and responsibility 2. To be knowledgeable and professional

Part I Lead-in

Question:

(1) How to greet the passengers when they are boarding?

(2) How to help passengers arrange their baggage in the cabin?

(3) How to arrange seats for passengers in the cabin?

Part II Background Information

欢迎词是乘务员和旅客正式沟通的开始，是客舱播音的序曲，一般由称谓、正文和结语三部分构成。欢迎词要有针对性，重点始终是乘客，乘务员的目标是把乘客凝聚在一起并拥有共同的核心目标。欢迎词具有礼仪性和介绍性，要简洁明了、热情洋溢。

Part III Let's Read

Good morning, ladies and gentlemen,

Welcome aboard Air China Flight CA4117 from Chengdu to Beijing (via Xi'an). The distance between Chengdu and Beijing is 1 982 kilometers. Our flight will take 3 hours and 35 minutes. We will be flying at the altitude of 10 000 meters and the average speed is 800 kilometers per hour.

In order to ensure the normal operation of aircraft navigation and communication systems, mobile phones and other electronic devices throughout the flight and the laptop computers are not allowed to use during take-off and landing.

We will take off soon. Please make sure that your seat belt is securely fastened and that you refrain from smoking during the flight.

On our flight today, the chief purser with all your crew members will be sincerely at your service.

We hope you will enjoy your flight. Thank you!

女士们，先生们，早上好！

　　欢迎您乘坐中国航空公司CA4117次航班，由成都前往北京（经由西安）。由成都至北京的飞行距离是1 982千米，预计空中飞行时间是3小时35分。飞行高度10 000米，飞行平均速度每小时800千米。

　　为了保障飞机导航及通信系统的正常工作，在飞机起飞和下降过程中请不要使用手提式电脑，在整个航程中请不要使用手提电话和其他的电子设备。

　　飞机很快就要起飞了，请您系好安全带，在整个旅途中请不要吸烟。

　　本次航班的乘务长协同机上其他乘务员竭诚为您服务。我们希望各位乘客享受此次飞行。谢谢！

Part IV　Words and Expressions

1. via /ˈvaɪə/ *prep.* 取道；通过
2. altitude /ˈæltɪtjuːd/ *n.* 高度；海拔；飞行高度
3. average /ˈæv(ə)rɪdʒ/ *adj.* 平均的；普通的
   average speed　平均速度
4. normal operation /ˈnɔːm(ə)l ˌɒpəˈreɪʃ(ə)n/ *n.* 常规操作
5. navigation /ˌnævɪˈɡeɪʃ(ə)n/ *n.* 导航；领航
6. communication /kəˌmjuːnɪˈkeɪʃ(ə)n/ *n.* 交流；交际；通信
7. system /ˈsɪstəm/ *n.* 系统
8. electronic /ˌɪlekˈtrɒnɪk/ *adj.* 电子的；电动的
9. device /dɪˈvaɪs/ *n.* 装置，设备
   electronic device　电子设备
10. refrain /rɪˈfreɪn/ *v.* 制止；避免；节制

Part V　Reading Skill

语音浊化
Voice Turbidity

　　浊化规则：爆破音的清辅音跟在音标/s/后面时，产生浊化现象；辅元连读时浊化：在同一个意群里，爆破音的清辅音前后都是元音时，产生浊化现象。

英语中，发生音浊化现象必须同时具备如下四个条件：在同一个重读音节或次重读音节内；一个清辅音前的音是/s/；该清辅音对应的浊辅音；该清辅音后还有元音。在同一个音节内，当一个清辅音前的音是/s/，那么，/s/后面的清辅音要浊化。

例如，discussion：把/k/浊化成/g/，因此不要读成 discu/kʌ/ssion。

同理，stand：/t/浊化成/d/不能读成 s/t/and。

expression：/p/浊化成/b/不能读成 ex/p/ression。

我们来看如下广播词里的例子。

① We expect to land there at 2:20.

② We sincerely appreciate your understanding.

③ Our aircraft is still on an active runway.

④ For your safety, please do not open overhead bin until the aircraft has come to a complete stop.

在美音中，/t/在单词的中间被浊化成/d/。例如，作家（writer）听起来和骑手（rider）的发音几乎没有区别。

Part VI Practical Practice

1. Match the expressions in Column A with their Chinese equivalents in Column B.

Column A   Column B

(1) electronic   a. 系统

(2) navigation   b. 导航

(3) device   c. 高度

(4) altitude   d. 设备

(5) system   e. 电子的

2. Translate the following sentences into English.

（1）我们的飞行高度为 10 000 米，飞行平均速度为每小时 800 千米。

（2）请您系好安全带，在整个旅途中请不要吸烟。

Task 6 Welcome Speech

3. Translate the following sentences into Chinese.

(1) On our flight today, the chief purser with all your crew members will be sincerely at your service.

(2) In order to ensure the normal operation of aircraft navigation and communication systems, laptop computers are not allowed to use during take-off and landing.

4. Practice oral English.

Ladies and gentlemen,

May I have your attention, please? Welcome aboard Hainan Airlines Flight HU7607. We are bound for Beijing on a Boeing 767 and the flight time is about 2 hours and 10 minutes. Please take your seat according to your seat number. Your hand baggage can be put in the overhead compartment or under the seat in front of you. Please don't put anything in the emergency exits. If you need any assistance, please contact our flight attendants. We will land in Beijing Capital International Airport Terminal 3.

Thank you!

Task 7
Flight Route Introduction

A man's politeness is a mirror that shows his portrait.
一个人的礼貌，就是一面照出他的肖像的镜子。

Learning Objectives
Knowledge Objectives
1. To know how to make an announcement of flight route introduction
2. To learn some useful expressions about flight route
Skill Objectives
1. To be able to get to know the key words and expressions
2. To be able to know the reading skills for flight information
Quality Objectives
1. To cultivate a rigorous and serious work attitude
2. To be knowledgeable and professional

Part I Lead-in

Question:

(1) How do the cabin attendants greet passengers?

(2) What contents does the Pre-flight briefing consist of?

Task 7 Flight Route Introduction

Part II Background Information

航线及服务介绍涉及了城市、距离、温度等内容的表达，还含有一些较难的生词。广播前提前了解飞行距离、飞行时间和代码共享等航线信息。广播短句建议依据广播词字符之间的空格来断句。例如，我谨代表全体机组/欢迎您搭乘/天合联盟成员/中国东方航空班机/前往×××。

Part III Let's Read

Ladies and gentlemen,

Welcome aboard Air China Flight CA1234. We have left Tianjin for Guangzhou. The distance between Tianjin and Guangzhou is _____ kilometers. Our flight will take 3 hours and 15 minutes, we expect to arrive at Guangzhou Baiyun International Airport at 14:20.

（Along this route, we will be flying over the provinces of _____, across over the _____.）

For your safety, we strongly recommend that you keep your seat belt fastened at all times, as there may be unexpected turbulence in flight.

Breakfast and beverages have been prepared for you. If you need any assistance, please feel comfortable to contact any one of us.

We wish you a pleasant journey. Thank you!

女士们，先生们：

欢迎您乘坐中国国际航空公司 CA1234 航班。我们的飞机已经离开天津前往广州，由天津至广州的飞行距离是_____千米，飞行时间为 3 小时 15 分钟，预计到达广州白云国际机场的时间是 14:20。

沿着这条航线我们将经过_____省，我们还将飞越_____。

在飞行全程中可能会出现因气流变化而引起的突然颠簸，为了您的安全，我们强烈建议您，全程系好安全带。

旅途中，我们为您准备了早餐及各种饮料，如果您需要帮助，我们很乐意随时为您服务。

旅客朋友们，能伴您度过轻松愉快的旅程，是我们全体机组成员的荣幸，谢谢！

Part IV　Words and Expressions

1. fly over the river 在河面上飞行
   fly across the river 飞过那条河
   walk over the bridge 走在桥上
   walk across the bridge 通过那座桥

2. between _____ and _____ is _____ kilometers
   between...and...在……和……之间。between 只能表示"在两者之间"，既可以表示时间也可以表示位置。表示位置时，"在三者或三者以上之间/之中"要用 among
   from...to...从……到……既可表示时间也可表示距离

3. province /ˈprɒvɪns/ n. 省；范围；领域

4. recommend /ˌrekəˈmend/ v. 推荐；举荐

5. unexpected /ˌʌnɪkˈspektɪd/ adj. 意料不到的；突然的

6. turbulence /ˈtɜːbjələns/ n. 紊流，湍流；混乱；冲突

Part V　Reading Skill

飞行距离、飞行时间和代码共享等航线信息的朗读技巧

Reading Skills for Flight Information such as Flight Distance, Flight Time and Code Sharing

一般而言，关于飞行距离、飞行时间和代码共享等航线信息的朗读技巧，广播时依据广播词字符之间的空格来断句。

例如，我谨代表全体机组/ 欢迎您搭乘/ 天合联盟成员/中国东方航空班机/前往（　　）。

Task 7 Flight Route Introduction

英语知识点 1：飞行时间表达

e.g. 2 小时 30 分钟

Two hours and thirty minutes

e.g. 1 小时 40 分钟

One hour and forty minutes

one hour 要连读。

相邻两个词，前者以辅音音素结尾，后者以元音音素开头，往往要拼在一起连读。

因此 one hour 的读法为/wʌn aʊr/。

英语知识点 2：飞行距离表达

e.g. 8 486 千米

Eight thousand four hundred and eighty-six kilometers

Part VI Practical Practice

1. Match the expressions in Column A with their Chinese equivalents in Column B.

Column A

(1) distance

(2) assistance

(3) turbulence

(4) recommend

(5) journey

Column B

a. 举例

b. 建议

c. 颠簸

d. 旅程

e. 协助

2. Translate the following sentences into English.

（1）由天津至上海的飞行距离是 1 080 千米。

（2）旅途中，我们为您准备了正餐及各种饮料。

3. Translate the following sentences into Chinese.

(1) For your safety, we strongly recommend that you keep your seat belt fastened at all times, as there may be unexpected turbulence in flight.

(2) If you need any assistance, please feel comfortable to contact any one of us.

4. Practice oral English.

(1) Ladies and gentlemen,

We have just left _____ for _____. During our trip, we shall provide the service of lunch with beverages. We have prepared newspapers, magazines for you. This aircraft has audio system, you can use the earphone to choose what you like.

Our captain is a pilot with rich flying experiences. As a result, his perfect flying skills will ensure you a safe journey. Meanwhile, we have rich working experiences, and will take care of the special passengers. To ensure your safety during the flight, we advise you to fasten your seatbelt while seated. If you have any needs or requirements, please let us know.

Wish you a pleasant journey!

Thank you!

(2) Ladies and gentlemen,

This is your purser speaking. Welcome aboard _____ Airlines.

The plane you are taking is Airbus 320. Now we are going to _____, the whole flight takes about _____ hours _____ minutes. We will be landing at our destination at _____ (time). This is our golden flight. According to the regulation of CAAC, to be safe, we will provide cabin service after take-off 20 minutes. Today we have prepared lunch and several beverages.

We have prepared some nice items for you. Please enjoy your shopping time later. For your convenience of travel, you can get the application forms of _____ Club and comment card from our cabin crew.

We may encounter some turbulence, please fasten your seatbelt when you are seated. And make the seatbelt outside your blanket to avoid being bothered.

We wish you a pleasant journey!

Thank you!

Task 8
Safety Check Broadcast

Rome is not built in a day.
冰冻三尺，非一日之寒。

Learning Objectives
Knowledge Objectives
1. To know how to make an announcement of security inspection
2. To learn some useful words and expressions
Skill Objectives
1. To be able to use the key words and expressions on security inspection
2. To be able to know reading skill of types and training of cabin broadcast
Quality Objectives
1. To develop the sense of professionalism and fighting spirit
2. To be knowledgeable and professional

Part I Lead-in

Question:

Passengers taking flight all expect to have a smooth journey. However, emergency or special situations do sometimes happen whether they like it or not, so safety check is very important.

As a flight attendant, you are doing safety check in the cabin before take-off.

The plane is going to take off. However, a passenger wants to go to the lavatory. How would you do?

Part II Background Information

当旅客登机的时候，先播放登机音乐，各个号位的乘务人员要站在各自的号位上用鞠躬礼和敬语迎接旅客登机。在旅客登机的同时，要向旅客介绍各号码对应的座位所在，协助旅客安放行李，帮助老幼病残孕旅客找到座位，整理行李架上的行李，并随时注意旅客的任何需要。旅客全部登机完毕之后，空乘人员通过演示或录像向旅客介绍客舱安全规定，内容包括：安全带的操作、氧气面罩的储藏位置及使用方法、吸烟的规定和救生衣的介绍。

Part III Let's Read

1. 起飞前安全检查

Ladies and gentlemen,

Now, please fasten your seat belts, stow your tray table, return your footrest to its initial position and put your seat back to the upright position. Please help us by opening the sunshades.

To ensure the safe operation of the navigation system, please make sure your cell phones, including those with flying mode, are switched off. This is a non-smoking flight, please do not smoke on board. We hope you enjoy the flight. Thank you!

Task 8　Safety Check Broadcast

女士们，先生们：

现在，请您将安全带系好，收起座椅靠背、小桌板及脚踏板，遮光板保持在打开的状态。

为了避免干扰通信导航系统的正常工作，确认您的手机及具有"飞行模式"功能的所有电子设备已经处于关闭状态。

我们提醒您：本次航班全程禁烟，敬请谅解！

祝您旅途愉快。谢谢！

2. 落地前安全检查

Ladies and gentlemen,

We are beginning our final descent. Please fasten your seatbelts, return your seat back to the upright position and stow your tray table, and return your footrest to its initial position. Please help us by opening the sunshades. All laptop computers and electronic devices should be turned off at this time. We kindly remind you that during landing and taxiing, please keep your seatbelts fastened and do not open the overhead compartment. We will be dimming the cabin lights for landing. Thank you!

女士们，先生们：

我们的飞机已经开始下降。请您将安全带系好，收起座椅靠背、小桌板及脚踏板，遮光板保持在打开的状态。请您关闭手提电脑及其他电子设备。我们善意地提醒您，在飞机着陆及滑行期间，请不要解开安全带或打开行李架。稍后，我们将调暗客舱灯光。

谢谢！

Part IV　Words and Expressions

1. footrest /ˈfʊtrɛst/ *n.* 搁脚物；脚蹬

2. initial /ɪˈnɪʃ(ə)l/ *adj.* 最初的；开始的

3. sunshade /ˈsʌnʃeɪd/ *n.* 阳伞；凉篷；遮光板

4. navigation /nævɪˈgeɪʃn/ *n.* 航行；航海；航空

5. descent /dɪˈsent/ *n.* 下降；下落

6. remind /rɪˈmaɪnd/ *v.* 使记起；使想起

7. compartment /kəmˈpɑːtmənt/ *n.* 船舱；隔间；车厢

Part V Reading Skill

客舱播音的类型与训练
Types and Training of Cabin Broadcast

在服务方面，通过广播让乘客了解此次航班的航程，时间，途经的省市和山脉、河流，还有其他一些服务项目。在安全方面，主要包括正常的安全检查，在起飞和落地前通过广播提醒乘客，还有在遇到特殊情况和突发事件时，通过广播以便让乘客了解情况。

（1）迎、送致辞：这类播音主要是欢迎和欢送乘客上、下飞机时常用的播音。要求语言清晰、亲切。

（2）客舱安全介绍：这类播音主要是对飞机上安全设备和安全措施以及注意事项进行介绍。要求语言庄重、规范、清晰、流畅。

（3）航线及注意事项介绍：这是客舱播音中最为普遍的，需要熟练掌握并且保证内容精确无误。

（4）风光导入类型：空乘人员经常需要承担起导游的角色，主动介绍途经的名胜古迹。这种播音要求信息准确、富有感情色彩。

（5）特殊情况播音：遇到气流飞机颠簸、飞机延误、备降等情况时，乘务员的播音一定要及时、自信、沉稳。

Part VI Practical Practice

1. Match the expressions in Column A with their Chinese equivalents in Column B.

Column A   Column B
(1) operation   a. 笔记本电脑
(2) initial   b. 运转
(3) dim   c. 最初的
(4) mode   d. 模式
(5) laptop   e. （使）昏暗

2. Translate the following sentences into English.

（1）本次航班全程禁烟，敬请谅解！

（2）为了您的安全，在飞机着陆及滑行期间，请不要解开安全带或打开行李架。

3. Translate the following sentences into Chinese.

(1) To ensure the safe operation of the navigation system, please make sure your cell phones, including those with flying mode, are switched off.

(2) All laptop computers and electronic devices should be turned off at this time.

4. Practice oral English.

(1) Ladies and gentlemen,

Now the plane will be taking off and the flight attendants will do safety check. Please fasten your seatbelts, stow your tray table, return your footrest to its initial position and put your seat back to the upright position. Please help us by opening the sunshades. Your cooperation will be appreciated.

Thank you.

(2) Ladies and gentlemen,

Welcome aboard flight _____ from _____ to _____. Would you please check your ticket and boarding pass again to make sure you're boarding the right flight?

As you enter the cabin, we kindly ask you that please take your seat as soon as possible to give room for other passengers who may be standing in the aisle behind you.

Your seat number is indicated on the bottom edge of the overhead baggage compartment. Please place your carry-on baggage in the overhead compartment.

Small or fragile baggage should be placed under the seat in front of you.

Please do not leave any baggage either in the aisle or near an exit door.

Thank you for your cooperation!

Task 9
Emergency Exit

Virtue is fairer far than beauty.

美德远远胜过美貌。

Learning Objectives
Knowledge Objectives 1. To know how to make an announcement about emergency exit 2. To learn some useful expressions about emergency exit **Skill Objectives** 1. To be able to master the key words and expressions 2. To be able to know to have an informative voice **Quality Objectives** 1. To develop the awareness of security and responsibility 2. To be knowledgeable and professional

Part I Lead-in

Question:

CA: Excuse me, sir. I'm sorry to interrupt you. You are sitting at the emergency exit. May I introduce the Safety Instruction for you now?

PAX: All right.

Do you know how to introduce emergency exit to the passengers?

Part II　Background Information

无论是在实际飞行中，还是在英语综合能力测试中，用英文介绍紧急出口都是必不可少的。我们接下来介绍如何用英文介绍飞机上的紧急出口。

介绍紧急出口的关键点：

（1）评定该旅客是否可以坐在紧急出口处。

（2）向旅客介绍紧急出口的使用方法并让其监控紧急出口的状态。

（3）向旅客介绍紧急出口小桌板的使用方法及对出口行李的要求。

（4）询问旅客是否听懂以及是否愿意坐在这里。

（5）旅客如果愿意坐在紧急出口处，请旅客阅读安全须知并且表示感谢；如果不愿意，帮助旅客调换座位。

Part III　Let's Read

1. 飞机关门后、插放安全须知视频前广播

Good morning/ afternoon/ evening, ladies and gentlemen,

　　To be safe, we will show you the location of the emergency exits.

　　There are six / eight / ten emergency exits located at the forward, rear and middle of the cabin.

We will show you safety demonstration video and appreciate your attention.

Thank you!

女士们，先生们：

早上/下午/晚上好！

为了确保安全，我们为您介绍紧急出口的位置：

客舱内共有 6 / 8 / 10 个紧急出口，分别位于客舱的前部、后部和中部。

接下来，我们将为您播放安全须知，敬请关注。谢谢！

2. 紧急出口位置介绍

Ladies and gentlemen,

To be safe, we will show you the location of the emergency exits.

There are _____(six/ eight/ ten) emergency exits located at the forward, middle and rear of the cabin. We will show you safety demonstration video and appreciate your attention.

女士们，先生们：

为了确保安全，我们为您介绍紧急出口的位置。客舱内共有_____（6/8/10）个紧急出口，分别位于客舱的前部、中部和后部。接下来，我们将为您播放安全须知，请您仔细观看。

Part IV　Words and Expressions

1. location /ləʊˈkeɪʃn/ *n.* 位置；场所

    the location of ……的位置

    look for the location (for) 寻找（……的）位置

    pinpoint a location 精确地指出位置

    secure the location 确定地点

2. emergency /ɪˈmɜːdʒənsɪ/ *n.* 突然事件；紧急情况

    emergency exit 紧急出口

3. rear /rɪə(r)/ *n.* 后面

    the rear seat belts in a car 汽车后座安全带

    a rear entrance/window 后门/后窗

    the offside rear wheel 外侧后轮

Part V　Reading Skill

客舱播音的强调处理
An Informative Voice

朗读这些广播时，我们要避免过于情绪化，应该保持正式而权威的声调，通过广播传达安全的信息。处理在客舱播音的过程中涉及的一些动词、名词时，如机门、关闭、旅客、就座、离机等词汇，注意音准，语气亲切，使用适中的自然语速，播音咬字清晰。我们强调处理的方式有重读、高调、延音等。广播要注意积极、大方、主动，使广播播音显得稳重、大方。克服吐字发音的不良习惯，在现有发声条件的基础上发挥长处、克服短处，扩展发声能力，找到自己最好的声音，逐渐克服"压、挤、捏、喧、憋"的错误用气发声状态。

Part VI　Practical Practice

1. Match the expressions in Column A with their Chinese equivalents in Column B.

　　Column A　　　　　　　　　　Column B
(1) location　　　　　　　　　　a. 紧急情况
(2) emergency　　　　　　　　　b. 位置
(3) entrance　　　　　　　　　　c. 入口
(4) exit　　　　　　　　　　　　d. 最后的
(5) rear　　　　　　　　　　　　e. 出口

2. Translate the following sentences into English.

（1）客舱内共有6个紧急出口，分别位于客舱的前部、后部和中部。

（2）为了您的安全，我们将为您介绍紧急出口的位置。

3. Translate the following sentences into Chinese.

(1) We will show you safety demonstration video and appreciate your attention.

(2) If the exit cannot be used, move to another one immediately.

4. Practice oral English.

Ladies and gentlemen,

Now the flight attendants will tell you the location of your nearest exit. Please ensure two exits at least. Follow the instructions of the flight attendants and do not take anything while evacuating. If the exit cannot be used, move to another one immediately.

Task 10
Fasten the Seat Belt

No cross, no crown.
不经历风雨，怎么见彩虹。

微课抢先看

Learning Objectives
Knowledge Objectives
1. To know how to make an announcement about how to fasten the seat belt
2. To learn some useful expressions about fastening the seat belt
Skill Objectives
1. To be able to conduct an announcement about seat belt
2. To be able to read rhythmically and perform at the workplace
Quality Objectives
1. To develop the awareness of security and responsibility
2. To be knowledgeable and professional

Part I Lead-in

Question:

(1) How do the passengers have to fasten their seat belts?

(2) Have you ever heard of the most dangerous "11 minutes" while in the flight?

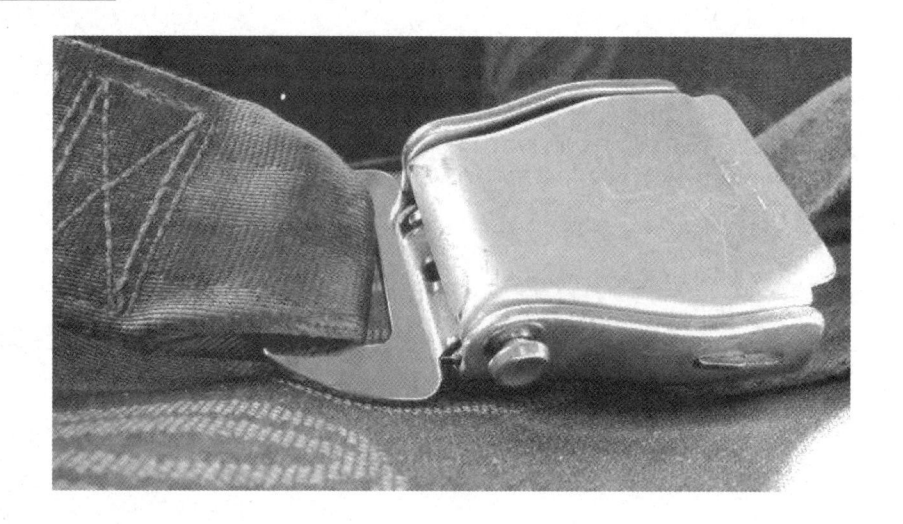

Part II Background Information

安全带是装在座椅骨架上的一条不起眼的带子。你可不要小看它，认为它像我们的腰带一样，想怎么使用就怎么使用，系紧点儿、系松点儿都不要紧，甚至不喜欢用就不用。其实这条小小的带子，在飞机飞行中或起降过程的关键时候，起着约束你的身体、确保人身安全的大作用。特别是在紧急着陆的情况下，它甚至可以保住你的生命。因此，在客机从机场起飞、平飞到安全着陆之前的整个飞行过程中，不论你正在客舱中做什么，只要客机上系好安全带的警示灯一亮或者空乘提示后，你就应该立刻回到自己的座位上坐好，并系好安全带。

Part III Let's Read

1. Each chair has a seat belt that must be fastened when you are seated. Please keep your seat belt securely fastened during the whole flight. If needed, you may release the seat belt by pulling the flap forward. You can adjust it when necessary.

每位旅客座椅上都有一条安全带，请您落座后将安全带扣好。请全程系紧安全带。如需要解开，只需要将金属扣向外打开即可。您可以根据需要自行调节长度。

When the Fasten Seat Belt sign is illuminated, please fasten your seat belt. To fasten your seat belt, simply place the metal tip into the buckle and tighten the strap. To release, just lift up the top of the buckle.

当"系好安全带"灯亮时，请系好安全带。系好安全带只需您将金属片放进锁扣里，然后系紧带子。解开时，将锁扣打开，拉出金属片。

Task 10 Fasten the Seat Belt

2. Good morning, ladies and gentlemen,

Our plane is descending now. Please be seated and fasten your seat belt. Seat backs and tables should be returned to the upright position. All personal computers and electronic devices should be turned off. And please make sure that your carry-on items are securely stowed. We will be dimming the cabin lights for landing. Thank you!

女士们，先生们：

飞机正在下降。请您回原位坐好，系好安全带，收起小桌板，将座椅靠背调整到正常位置。所有个人电脑及电子设备应该处于关闭状态。请您确认您的手提物品是否已妥善安放。稍后，我们将调暗客舱灯光。

谢谢！

3. Good afternoon, ladies and gentlemen,

We expect to land at 8:00 P.M. on Beijing Capital International Airport. Please fasten your seat belt.

I would like to thank you for flying with China airlines.

I do hope you have enjoyed your flight.

女士们，先生们，午安：

我们预计下午 8 点降落在北京首都国际机场。请系好您的安全带。本人谨代表中国航空公司及全体组员感谢您的搭乘并祝您旅途愉快！

Part IV Words and Expressions

1. seatbelt /siːtbelt/ n.（汽车、飞机的）座椅安全带

2. flat /flæt/ n.（附于某物的）封盖，口盖，袋盖

3. adjust /əˈdʒʌst/ v. 调整；调节

4. illuminate /ɪˈluːmɪneɪt/ v. 照明；照亮；照射

5. buckle /ˈbʌkl/ n.（皮带等的）搭扣，搭钩

6. strap /stræp/ n. 带子

7. upright /ˈʌpraɪt/ adj. 竖直的；直立的；垂直的

8. dim /dɪm/ v. 变暗淡，变微弱，变昏暗

Part V Reading Skill

学会有节奏的朗读
Learn to Read Rhythmically

英语的节奏是指英语音节在语流中强读和弱读的规律性。它以"步"（foot）为基础，每句话都有若干"步"，就好像音乐中的"小节"（bar）一样，每段乐曲都含有若干个小节。乐曲中每个小节一般以强拍开始。英语中，一般来说，每一"步"的第一个音节都是重读音节。有的"步"由单独一个重读音节组成，有的"步"由一个重读音节加上若干非重读音节组成。在朗读中，有的"步"有时也能以非重读音节开始，就如乐曲中的小节以休止符开始一样。这个"步"的非重读音节前也有个休止符，被称为 silent beat。现在，我们用"/"表示"步"与"步"之间的界线，例如：

(1) one/two/three/four/five.

(2) the/first of/April/nineteen/seventy/one/.

每个人说话的速度不同，同一个人在不同的环境条件、不同的情绪下说话的快慢也各不相同。然而，在采用某一种语速的过程中，每"步"所需要的时间大致上是相等的，就像音乐中每个小节所占的时间相等一样，这就形成了节奏。为了保持节奏，包含音节多的语速就必须比包含音节少的语速快一些。因此，朗读时就必须懂得英语的节奏，自觉地实践。

Part VI Practical Practice

1. Match the expressions in Column A with their Chinese equivalents in Column B.

Column A   Column B
(1) upright   a. 垂直的
(2) dim   b. 照亮
(3) illuminate   c. 搭扣
(4) buckle   d. 调整
(5) adjust   e. （使）变暗淡

2. Translate the following sentences into English.

（1）请系好您的安全带。

（2）每位旅客的座椅上都有一条安全带。

3. Translate the following sentences into Chinese.

(1) If needed, you may release the seat belt by pulling the flap forward.

(2) You can adjust it when necessary.

4. Practice oral English.

(1) Ladies and gentlemen,

We will show you the use of lite vest, oxygen mask, seat belt and the location of the emergency exits. Please give us your full attention for the demonstration.

Your oxygen mask is stored in the compartment above your head, and it will drop automatically in case of emergency. When the mask drops, pull it towards you to cover your mouth and nose, and slip the elastic band over your head, and then breathe normally.

(2) Ladies and gentlemen,

We have landed at Beijing Capital International Airport, please remain seated until the "FASTEN SEAT BELT" sign is turned off and the aircraft has come to a complete stop. Please don't forget to take along your personal belongings. When opening the overhead bins, please take care to ensure the contents do not fall out. Once again, we would like to thank you for flying with China Airlines and hope to serve you again soon.

Task 11

Safety Demonstration

Lies can never change fact.

谎言终究是谎言。

Learning Objectives
Knowledge Objectives
1. To know how to make an announcement safety demonstration
2. To learn some useful expressions about safety demonstration
Skill Objectives
1. To be able to master the key words and expressions
2. To be able to know the labor-saving technique (omitted)
Quality Objectives
1. To develop the sense of safety awareness and professionalism
2. To be knowledgeable and professional

Part I Lead-in

Question:

(1) What are the safety demonstration items in the cabin?

(2) Do you know how to explain the uses of safety demonstration items to passengers?

Task 11　Safety Demonstration

Part II　Background Information

飞行前的安全演示是指起飞前乘务员为乘客做关于本次航班安全特性的详细解释和说明。安全示范的标准是按国际民航组织和中国民用航空局制定的国际航空安全准则来执行的。在小型飞机上，安全演示是采用现场演示的方式进行的。一名乘务员站在过道上演示，另一名乘务员通过公共广播系统进行解释说明。如今，许多大型飞机配备了机上娱乐设备，安全演示大多会采用视频的形式为旅客播放，一般持续 2~6 分钟。考虑到乘客语言或听力障碍，视频还可能会有字幕或不同语言的翻译。安全演示的内容通常包括安全带、氧气面罩和救生衣的使用方式、防冲撞姿势、示范电子设备的限制使用、行李的妥善放置、安全出口的位置、禁止吸烟、起飞前的准备等方面。

Part III　Let's Read

Ladies and gentlemen,

　　Our flight attendants will now demonstrate the use of the life vest, oxygen mask and seatbelt, and show you the location of the emergency exits.

　　Your life vest is located under your seat. Slip the life-vest over your head.

　　Bring the waist strap around our waist. Fasten the buckles and tighten it by pulling it outwards.

To inflate your life vest, pull firmly on the red cord, only when leaving the aircraft.

To inflate further, blow into these mouthpieces.

Your oxygen mask is located in a compartment above your seat. It will drop automatically in case of decompression.

Pull a mask down sharply to activate the flow of oxygen. Place the mask over your nose and mouth. Pull the elastic strap over your head and tighten it by pulling the end of the strap. In a few seconds, the oxygen will begin to flow.

Your seatbelt contains two pieces. To fasten the belt, slip one piece into the buckle and tighten it.

Please keep your seatbelts securely fastened when seated.

女士们，先生们：

现在客舱乘务员向您展示救生衣、氧气面罩、安全带的使用方法和应急出口的位置。

救生衣在您座椅下面的口袋里，使用时取出，经头部穿好。

将腰带在腰间系紧扣上扣环，向外拉紧。

给救生衣充气，只有离开飞机时才能拉紧红色绳子。

充气不足时，用嘴向人工充气管里充气。

氧气面罩位于您座椅的上方，发生紧急情况时面罩会自动脱落。

氧气面罩脱落后，请用力向下拉面罩。

将面罩罩在口鼻处，把松紧带套在头上通过拉动带子下端系紧松紧带。几秒钟后，就会有氧气供应。

您的安全带分为两部分。将带子插进带扣，然后拉紧。

当您就座时，请确保系好安全带。

Part IV   Words and Expressions

1. demonstrate /ˈdɛmənˌstreɪt/ *vt.* 证明；演示；说明

2. oxygen /ˈɑːksɪdʒən/ *n.* [化] 氧，氧气

3. waist /weɪst/ *n.* 腰，腰部

4. inflate /ɪnˈfleɪt/ *vt.& vi.* （使）充气

5. automatically /ˌɔtəˈmætɪklɪ/ *adv.* 自动地

6. decompression /ˌdikəmˈprɛʃən/ *n.* 减压，解压；失压

7. activate /ˈæktəˌvet/ *vt.* 使活动；起动；触发

8. elastic /ɪˈlæstɪk/ *adj.* 有弹力的；可伸缩的

Part V Reading Skill

省力技巧
Labor-saving Technique (omitted)

略音也被称为"省音",省音也就是"秘力"(也叫不完全爆破),是一种常见的音变现象。在自然流利的谈话中,为了说话省力,经常把一些音省掉。省音既可出现在单词内,也可出现在词与词之间。

某单词字尾是辅音,而后面相邻的单词开头也是辅音,并且词头、词尾的两个辅音相同时,两个相同的辅音只读一个即可;也就是省前读后。

例如,Keep quiet!

Take care!

I had a good time last night.

辅音+辅音——同性相斥。在以/t/、/d/、/k/、/g/、/p/+以辅音开始的单词时,前面的辅音发音顿息,舌头达到发音部位"点到为止",但不送气!在正常速度或快速的对话中,字尾有/t/、/d/时通常不会把/t/、/d/的发音清楚地念出来,而是快要念出来时,马上憋气顿息,因此字尾/t/、/d/的发音常常是听不到的。

例如,I don't know what to do.

I need some more money.

We expect to arrive at Guangzhou Baiyun International Airport at 14:20.

Part VI Practical Practice

1. Match the expressions in Column A with their Chinese equivalents in Column B.

Column A   Column B

(1) demonstrate   a. 使充气

(2) inflate   b. 氧气

(3) oxygen   c. 演示

(4) elastic   d. 有弹力的

(5) automatically   e. 自动地

2. Translate the following sentences into English.

(1)氧气面罩位于您座椅的上方。

（2）当您就座时，请系好安全带。

3. Translate the following sentences into Chinese.

(1) Your life vest is located under your seat.

(2) It will drop automatically in case of decompression.

4. Practice oral English.

(1) Ladies and gentlemen,

We will now take a moment to explain how to use the onboard emergency equipment and locate the exits.

Your life vest is located under/ above your seat. It can only be used in case of ditching. Please do not remove it unless instructed by your flight attendant.

To put your vest on, simply slip it over your head, then fasten the buckles and pull the straps tightly around your waist.

Upon exiting the aircraft, pull the tabs down firmly to inflate your vest. Please do not inflate your vest while inside the cabin. For further inflation, simply blow into the mouth pieces on either side of your vest.

For ditching at night, a sea-light will be illuminated automatically.

Thank you.

(2) Ladies and gentlemen,

Now the flight attendants will tell you the location of your nearest exit. Please ensure two exits at least. Follow the instructions of the flight attendants and do not take anything while evacuating. If the exit cannot be used, move to another one immediately.

(3) Ladies and gentlemen,

May I have your attention please for the video of safety demonstration? If you have any questions, please contact our flight attendants.

Thank you.

Task 12
Life Vest

Knowledge makes humble, ignorance makes proud.
博学使人谦逊，无知使人骄傲。

Learning Objectives
Knowledge Objectives
1. To know how to make an announcement about life vest
2. To learn some useful expressions about life vest
Skill Objectives
1. To be able to master the key words and expressions
2. To be able to learn to read the intonation
Quality Objectives
1. To develop the awareness of safety and professionalism
2. To be knowledgeable and professional

Part I Lead-in

Question:

There are two colors of life jackets on the plane: yellow and red. Among them, red is for crew use, and yellow is for passenger use. These two colors are warning colors, which make rescuers easy to find and distinguish in the vast sea. So, how to use life jackets on airplanes?

Part II Background Information

飞机上的救生衣不是降落伞。根据规定，飞机在海上飞行时是需要具备救生衣等救生装备的，但没有配置降落伞。飞机上的救生衣是为了飞机发生紧急情况需要降落到水面的时候，用来水上求生的工具，起到了保护乘客人身安全的作用。救生衣不仅仅是帮助落水者自救，在飞机失事时，会起到更大的作用。救生衣一般会采用鲜艳且显眼的颜色，目的是让救援人员在飞机坠毁地点较易发现坠机人员的方位。救生衣分为红色和黄色两种，红色的供机组人员使用，黄色的则提供给乘客。如果在低温或强风的地带，救生衣还能起到一定的保暖作用。

Part III Let's Read

Ladies and gentlemen,

  The life vest on board can only be used under emergency situation. Under normal situation, any action of removal, takeaway is forbidden. Your compliance of the rule is appreciated. Thank you!

女士们，先生们：

  机上救生衣属于飞机应急救生设备，仅供紧急情况下使用。在飞机正常运行中，任何随意移动甚至将救生衣带离飞机的行为都将被禁止。请大家遵守并配合客舱的安全工作。谢谢！

Task 12 Life Vest

Now the flight attendants will explain the use of life vest. Please take your life vest on and follow the instruction of your flight attendants.

现在我们将向您介绍救生衣的使用方法。请按照乘务员指导穿上您的救生衣。

Your life vest is located under your seat.

救生衣在您座位底下。

Pull the tab to open the pouch and remove the life vest. To put the vest on, slip it over your head.

拉动标签并撕开包装,取出救生衣并将其经头部穿好。

Then fasten the buckles and pull the straps tight around your waist.

然后将带子绕过腰间系紧。

Upon leaving the aircraft, inflate your life vest by pulling down on the two red tabs, but do not inflate it while you are in the cabin.

当您离开飞机时,拉动救生衣两侧的红色充气把手,但在客舱内不要充气。

If your life vest needs further inflation, you can pull the mouthpieces from the upper part of the vest and blow into them.

充气不足时,可将救生衣上部人工充气管拉出,用嘴向里吹气。

Your flight attendants will help any passenger who needs assistance.

乘务员将协助任何需要帮助的旅客穿上救生衣。

Additional information

补充信息

(1) Life vests can only be used in case of emergency. Please do not use life jackets in normal circumstances. (There have been cases in which passengers take out the life vests under their seat and inflate it quickly after listening to the demonstration and explaining how to use the emergency equipment on board).

救生衣只有在紧急情况时才使用,正常情况请不要使用救生衣。(出现过旅客在乘务员演示讲解如何使用机上应急设备知识后,把自己座位底下的救生衣拿出并迅速将其充气的案例。)

(2) Life vests belong to on-board emergency equipment, and cannot be taken off the aircraft when boarding. (Taking life vests off the aircraft is not only endangering the safety of other passengers, but also violating relevant laws and regulations).

救生衣属于机上应急设备,乘机时不能带下飞机。(将救生衣带下飞机不仅危及其他乘客的安全,更有可能触犯相关法律法规。)

Part IV Words and Expressions

1. vest /vest/ *n.* 马甲；背心
   life vest 救生衣
2. tab /tæb/ *n.* 标签；手柄
3. inflate /ɪnˈfleɪt/ *v.* 使充气；膨胀
4. blow /bləʊ/ *v.* 吹
5. removal /rɪˈmuːvl/ *n.* 免职；除去；移走；搬迁
6. compliance /kəmˈplaɪəns/ *n.* 遵守；服从
7. circumstance /ˈsɜːkəmstəns/ *n.* 条件；环境
8. violate /ˈvaɪəleɪt/ *v.* 违反；侵犯；打搅

Part V Reading Skill

语调

Intonation

发音纯正，读准了单词，但语调不对，不但听起来不舒服，甚至让人难以听懂说话人的意思。相反，如果语调正确，个别单词读不准，听起来像英语调子，还是能让人从语调上猜出说话人的意思的。因此，语调比发音更重要。语调是说话的腔调，是一句话里语音高低轻重的配置。英语语调主要表现在句子重音和声调上。语调不同，表达意思也各异。例如，She is a baby doctor. 如果仅重读 baby 这个词，意思是"她是儿科医生"；如果同时还重读 doctor 则表示"她是没有经验的医生"（quite young and unexperienced doctor）。又如，thank you 如果读成降调则表示感谢；如果读成升调，则毫无感谢之意，有时甚至表示反感。读准语调就是要读准句子的重音和声调，以及能抑扬顿挫地连读、弱读、失去爆破、同化等。在朗读时，应认真模仿英语录音提供的标准语调，坚持练习，使正确的语音、语调牢牢地被记住，以保证今后一开口就能读得对、读得准。

Part VI Practical Practice

1. Match the expressions in Column A with their Chinese equivalents in Column B.

   Column A   Column B
   (1) life vest   a. 手柄

(2) tab   b. 使充气
(3) inflate   c. 救生衣
(4) blow   d. 吹
(5) forbidden   e. 禁止

2. Translate the following sentences into English.

（1）在飞机正常运行时，任何随意移动甚至将救生衣带离飞机的行为都将被禁止。

（2）请大家遵守我们的规章制度并配合客舱的安全工作。

3. Translate the following sentences into Chinese.

(1) Upon leaving the aircraft, inflate your life vest by pulling down on the two red tabs.

(2) If your life vest needs further inflation, you can pull the mouthpieces from the upper part of the vest and blow into them.

4. Practice oral English.

(1) Ladies and gentlemen,

We will now take moment to explain how to use the emergency equipment and locate the exits.

Your life vest is located (under/ above) your seat. It may only be used in case of a water landing. Please do not remove it unless instructed by one of your flight attendants.

To put your vest on, simply slip it over your head. Then fasten the buckles and pull the straps tight around your waist.

Upon exiting the aircraft, pull the tabs down firmly to inflate your vest while inside the cabin. For further inflation, simply blow into the mouth pieces in either side of your vest.

For water landing at night, a sea-light will be illuminated.

For additional information, please review the safety instruction card in the seat pocket.

Now, please sit back and enjoy your flight. Thank you!

(2) Ladies and gentlemen,

We will now take a moment to explain how to use the onboard emergency equipment and locate the exits.

Your life vest is located under/ above your seat. It can only be used in case of ditching. Please do not remove it unless instructed by your flight attendant.

To put your vest on, simply slip it over your head, then fasten the buckles and pull the straps tightly around your waist.

Upon exiting the aircraft, pull the tabs down firmly to inflate your vest. Please do not inflate your vest while inside the cabin. For further inflation, simply blow into the mouth pieces on either side of your vest.

For ditching at night, a sea-light will be illuminated automatically.

Thank you.

Task 13
Smoking Prohibition

Reading is to the mind while exercise to the body.

读书健脑，运动强身。

微课抢先看

Learning Objectives
Knowledge Objectives
1. To be able to make an announcement about smoking prohibition
2. To be able to know the key words and expressions
Skill Objectives
1. To know how to make an announcement about smoking prohibition
2. To be able to know the reading skill of breath-holding training
Quality Objectives
1. To develop the sense of professional norms
2. To be knowledgeable and professional

Part I   Lead-in

Question:

(1) Do you smoke?

(2) If you smoke, would you like to give up?

(3) Can passengers be allowed to smoke in the cabin? If not, why?

Part II Background Information

中国民用航空局明确规定：航班全程禁烟，包括雾化电子烟。这样做的原因一是客舱高度封闭，空气不流通容易造成健康隐患；二是吸烟容易引起烟雾警报响起，造成恐慌，甚至可能造成难以控制而危及客舱安全的局面。此外，要明确一点，雾化电子烟也是烟，吸烟有害健康！雾化电子烟是一种模仿卷烟的电子产品，有着与卷烟一样的烟雾、味道和感觉。

Part III Let's Read

1. Good morning (afternoon/evening), ladies and gentlemen,

This is a non-smoking flight. According to the regulation of the Civil Aviation Administration of China, passengers are not allowed to smoke during the whole flight. Smoking or using E-cigarettes anywhere in the aircraft is against the law.

We will be taking-off immediately, please make sure that your seat belt is securely fastened.

Thank you for flying with us. Wish you a pleasant trip. Thank you!

女士们，先生们，早上好（下午好，晚上好）：

我们的航班全程禁止吸烟。根据中国民用航空局的规定，飞机上全程禁止吸烟，包括电子香烟在内的吸烟行为是违法的。

飞机马上就要起飞了，请您系好安全带。

谢谢您乘坐此次航班，祝您旅途愉快。谢谢！

2. Ladies and gentlemen,

Thank you for waiting, Flight CA985 for San Francisco is now ready for boarding. Passengers on

Task 13 Smoking Prohibition

this flight, please make their way to the gate No. 15. Please refrain from smoking beyond the gate! Thank you!

女士们，先生们，

感谢您在此等候。前往旧金山的 CA985 次航班，现已开始登机。请乘坐该航班的旅客到 15 号门登机。请勿在门外吸烟！谢谢！

3. Ladies and gentlemen,

In preparation for departure, we ask that you take your seats, place your seat in the upright position and fasten your seat belt securely. We also ask that you stow your small table and open the window shade.

This is a non-smoking flight. Smoking is not permitted in the cabin or lavatories. Tampering with or destroying the lavatory smoke detector is prohibited.

Thank you!

女士们，先生们：

飞机即将起飞，请您协助我们坐在座位上，调直座椅靠背，系好安全带。同时，请您收起小桌板，打开遮光板。

本次航班为禁烟航班。在客舱和盥洗室中禁止吸烟。严禁损坏盥洗室的烟雾探测器。

谢谢！

Part IV Words and Expressions

1. prohibition /ˌprəʊɪˈbɪʃn/ *n.* 禁止，阻止

2. non-smoking 无烟、禁烟的；不允许吸烟的

3. Civil Aviation Administration of China （CAAC）中国民用航空局

4. allow /əˈlaʊ/ *v.* 允许

5. permit /pəˈmɪt , ˈpɜːmɪt/ *v.* 允许；准许

6. cigarette /ˌsɪgəˈret/ *n.* 香烟；纸烟；卷烟
   e-cigarette 电子烟

7. upright /ˈʌpraɪt/ *adj.* 直立的；挺直的

8. stow /stəʊ/ *v.* 妥善放置；收好

9. lavatory /ˈlævətri/ *n.* 厕所，卫生间

10. detector /dɪˈtektə(r)/ *n.* 探测器，检测器
    smoke detector 烟雾探测器

Part V   Reading Skill

气息练习
Breath-holding Training

俗话说：练声先练气。气息是人体发声的动力和基础。在播音和主持时，气息的速度、流量、压力的大小与声音的高低、强弱、长短及共鸣情况都有直接关系。所谓"控制气息"，就是要学会胸腹联合呼吸法。气息练习的目的是为了体会和掌握胸腹联合呼吸的基本动作要领，形成新的、符合朗诵发声要求的呼吸方式。在生活中，人们的本能呼吸是浅呼吸，即只做胸部呼吸。播音或主持时，用这种本能呼吸的方法发音，时间一长，声带就会疲乏，声音就会嘶哑。而胸腹联合呼吸法，是要深呼吸，将空气吸入肺叶底部的横膈膜处，即一般人系腰带的地方。一般采用鼻子吸气，吸入横膈膜的气，使肋骨自然向外扩张。此时，腹部有发胀的感觉。随着小腹逐渐收缩，气息也从小腹深处涌上来，推动声带发音。通过这种方式发出的声音不仅洪亮、有力，而且持久，能保持整句话的声音都饱满圆润。气息练习方法有如下5种。

（1）软口盖练习法：最常见的是"闭口打哈欠"，即打哈欠时故意不张开嘴，而是强制用鼻子吸气、呼气。

（2）压腹数数法：平躺在床上，在腹部压上一摞书，吸足一口气，开始从1往后数。这是针对气息输出的强制训练，以达到增强腹肌和横膈膜的控气力度的目的。做这个练习时，开始阶段时压的书可少些，逐渐增加，即循序渐进。为了不占用工作中的时间，可利用睡前做这个练习。

（3）气声数数法：先吸足一口气，屏息数秒，然后用均匀的、低微的、带有气息的声音从1开始数数，就像是说悄悄话一样。与压腹数数法一样，在开始阶段可以数得少一点。不过应注意，数数时尽量不撒气、不漏气。

（4）跑步背诗法：平时跑步出现轻微气喘时，可背一首短小的古诗。开始训练时可两人配合进行，并肩小跑，一句接一句地背下去。

（5）偷气换气法：选一篇或一段长句较多的文章，用较快的速度读下去；在气息不足时，运用"偷气"技巧，读后确定最佳换气处。所谓"偷气"，是指不要边发声边吸气，而是要用极快的速度，在不为人觉察时吸入部分气流；而"换气"，宜口鼻并用，以鼻为主，掌握时间差，使气流充沛有力。

Task 13 Smoking Prohibition

Part VI Practical Practice

1. Match the expressions in Column A with their Chinese equivalents in Column B.

Column A   Column B
(1) permit   a. 香烟
(2) cigarette   b. 探测器
(3) refrain   c. 克制
(4) lavatory   d. 洗手间
(5) detector   e. 准许

2. Translate the following sentences into English.

（1）飞机马上就要起飞了，请您确认系好安全带。

（2）出门登机请勿吸烟！

3. Translate the following sentences into Chinese.

(1) According to the regulation of the Civil Aviation Administration of China, passengers are not allowed to smoke during the whole flight.

(2) Smoking is not permitted in the cabin or lavatories.

4. Practice oral English.

(1) Ladies and gentlemen,

The cabin door is closed. For your safety, please do not use your mobile phones and certain electronic devices on board at any time. Laptop computers may not be used during take-off and landing. Please ensure that your mobile phone is turned off. This is a non-smoking flight, please do not smoke on board.

Thank you for your cooperation!

(2) Ladies and gentlemen,

This is a non-smoking flight. Smoking onboard is an offence and is forbidden. Your cooperation is appreciated.

Thank you!

(3) Ladies and gentlemen,

We have a minor fire in the front (center/rear) cabin and we are quickly containing this situation. Please remain calm and follow the directions from your flight attendants. We will relocate the passengers near the fire. All other passengers remain seated with your seat belts fastened.

Thank you for your cooperation and assistance.

Task 14
Restrictions on Electronic Devices

Look before you leap.
三思而后行。

Learning Objectives
Knowledge Objectives
1. To know how to make an announcement about restrictions on electronic devices
2. To learn some useful expressions about restrictions on electronic devices
Skill Objectives
1. To be able to master the key words and expressions
2. To be able to know to cultivate breath control
Quality Objectives
1. To develop the awareness of standard and normative
2. To be knowledgeable and professional

Part I Lead-in

Question:

(1) Can passengers use cell phones during the fight?

(2) Can I use Bluetooth on an airplane?

(3) How to charge your device during a flight?

Part II Background Information

飞机起飞前,乘务员需要对客舱进行安全检查以确保飞机的正常运行和乘客的安全。

安全检查的内容主要包括：所有乘客是否已系好安全带；乘客的座椅靠背是否调直；机上的电子设备及手机是否关闭；乘客的行李是否已放置好；遮光板是否打开；小桌板是否收起等。安全检查程序完毕后飞机才能起飞。我们都知道,在飞机起降期间是严格限制使用电子设备的,《中华人民共和国民用航空法》及《民用航空飞行标准管理条例》中有严格的规定,针对在机上使用便携式电子设备并影响飞机起降安全的行为,予以治安管理处罚乃至刑事处罚！

Part III Let's Read

1. Ladies and gentlemen,

Welcome aboard _____ Airlines flight _____. Now the cabin door has been closed. To avoid interference with navigation system, please switch off your mobile phones and all electronic devices. Please fasten the seatbelts, ensure that your tables and seatbacks are in an upright position and open the window shades. Smoking is not allowed during the whole flight. We wish you a pleasant trip.

Thank you!

Task 14 Restrictions on Electronic Devices

女士们，先生们：

欢迎您乘坐_____航空公司的_____航班。现在舱门已经关闭，为了避免干扰通信导航系统，请您将手机和电子用品全部关闭。请您系好安全带，收起小桌板，调直座椅靠背并打开遮光板。本次航班全程禁烟，祝您旅途愉快！

谢谢！

2. Ladies and gentlemen,

Please note certain electronic devices must not be used on board at any time. These devices including cell phones, AM/FM radios, televisions and remote control equipment including toys. All other electronic devices including laptop computers and CD players must not be switched on until fifteen minutes after take-off, and must be switched off when the seatbelt signs come on for landing.

Your cooperation will be much appreciated.

女士们，先生们：

请注意，我们的航班上全程禁止使用电子设备，包括移动电话、收音机、电视及包括玩具在内的遥控电子设备。起飞后十五分钟内，笔记本电脑、CD 播放器等所有其他电子设备必须关闭。落地时，当安全带指示灯亮起，所有电子设备也必须关闭。

非常感谢您的合作！

Part IV Words and Expressions

1. restriction /rɪˈstrɪkʃən/ n. 限制；管制

2. electronic /ɪˌlekˈtrɒnɪk/ adj. 电子的

3. device /dɪˈvaɪs/ n. 装置；设备

4. cabin /ˈkæbɪn/ n. 客舱 cabin door 舱门

5. avoid /əˈvɔɪd/ v. 避免

6. interference /ˌɪntəˈfɪərəns/ n. 干扰

7. navigation /ˌnævɪˈgeɪʃən/ n. 导航
   navigation system 导航系统

8. turn off 把……关掉

9. mobile /ˈməʊbaɪl/ adj. 活动的；走动方便的
   mobile phone 移动电话

10. ensure /ɪnˈʃʊə/ vt. 确保

11. upright /ˈʌpraɪt/ adj. 垂直的

12. position /pəˈzɪʃən/ *n.* 位置

13. whole /həul/ *adj.* 全部的

14. pleasant /ˈplezənt/ *adj.* 令人愉快的

Part V Reading Skill

气息控制
Breath Control

气息控制对于播音主持者来说是非常重要的基本功，也是播音员业务素质的重要标准。气息控制可以缓解长时间播报给声带带来的压力，保持声音的圆润。练气发声的 4 种基本状态也可以用"稳、匀、细、活、深"5 个字来概括。

（1）声高气低。声音较高时，气息要深、沉、稳——支持点低。支持点低的感觉是得到骨盆的支持而产生的，气深压力大，有足够的动力保证，声带振动正常，效率高，能量大。

（2）声低气提。发低音时要有"提气"的感觉，更要注意保持吸气时各部位的状态。否则，发低音就很困难。

（3）声强气沉。声强要求气息压力大，必须在保持气柱深长的前提下，在丹田往上、往里收缩顶气的同时，使横膈膜和后腰处保持向下的力量。只有这样，气息才能平稳，压力大，从而保证强音的需要。

（4）声弱气稳。声音较弱时，仍然要保持稳劲的控制状态，从而保证声带振动相对稳定。否则，声弱气浮，声道不通，发音吃力，效果不好。

要注意纠正"气多声少"和"气少声多"的气、声不协调的毛病。

所谓"气多声少"，就是气息呼出量过大、过猛，超过了使声带正常振动所需的呼出量，而出现漏气现象。漏气不仅使声音粗糙，音色发沙、暗、空，而且由于发声效率低，声带负担重，容易受到损伤，损坏嗓子。

所谓"气少声多"，就是气息的呼出量过小，远远不足以使声带正常振动。在这种情况下，产生不了对抗的感觉，喉头负担重，声带容易受损。

呼气要不多不少，恰到好处，在对抗的感觉中得到保证和支持。

Part VI Practical Practice

1. Match the expressions in Column A with their Chinese equivalents in Column B.

Column A   Column B
(1) restriction   a. 导航

Task 14 Restrictions on Electronic Devices

(2) interference   b. 干扰

(3) upright   c. 位置

(4) position   d. 垂直的

(5) navigation   e. 限制

2. Translate the following sentences into English.

（1）请注意，某些电子设备在航班上禁止使用。

（2）祝您旅途愉快。

3. Translate the following sentences into Chinese.

(1) To avoid interference with navigation system, please switch off your mobile phones and all electronic devices.

(2) Please fasten the seatbelts, ensure that your tables and seatbacks are in an upright position and open the window shades.

4. Practice oral English.

Ladies and gentlemen,

Cabin doors have been closed. According to CAAC regulations, lithium power bank should be turned off. You may use your small portable electronic devices, such as mobile phones, after setting to airplane mode. Mobile phones without airplane mode, interphones and remote control equipment are prohibited during the entire flight. Headsets and oversized laptop or tablet PC are prohibited in critical flight phases, such as taxiing, take-off, descent and landing. In order to ensure flight safety, cigarette and equivalent smoking are prohibited in this flight.

Thank you.

Task 15
Transfer Flight Information

Do not teach fish to swim.

不要班门弄斧。

微课抢先看

Learning Objectives
Knowledge Objectives
1. To know how to make an announcement of transfer flight information
2. To learn some useful words and expressions
Skill Objectives
1. To be able to master the words and expressions
2. To be able to learn proper language
Quality Objectives
1. To develop the sense of customer first and standardized service
2. To be knowledgeable and professional

Part I Lead-in

Question:

1. Where should the transit passenger go through transfer formalities?

2. Which of the following items do belong to transfer procedures for international flight?

Task 15 Transfer Flight Information

Part II Background Information

因为多种原因，乘客往往无法直接飞到目的地。他们需要先飞到一个中转城市，然后转乘另一个班机去往目的地。常见的转机程序如下：

（1）国内转国内。如果已办理联程登机与行李直挂，可根据国内中转标识指引到达国内中转柜台，加盖中转印章后进入候机厅后登机。如果未办理联程登机手续，有随身行李的乘客需先提取行李再前往中转柜台办理登机和托运手续，完成后通过安检，之后进入候机厅登机。无随身行李的乘客直接到达国内中转柜台，办理登机牌并加盖中转印章后进入候机厅登机。

（2）国内转国际。首先提取行李（如有），前往国内转国际柜台，并在该柜台办理登机牌及行李托运，其次前往国际出发大厅，通过海关边防、检验检疫和安检后到达国际候机厅登机。

Part III Let's Read

1. Ladies and gentlemen,

We will be landing at Chengdu Shuangliu International Airport after about twenty minutes. Please be seated and fasten your seat belt. Seat backs and tables should be returned to the upright position. If you have a connecting flight, you'll have to go to the domestic terminal after you have declared Customs. It's just beside the international terminal. Thank you.

女士们，先生们：

我们将在大约 20 分钟后抵达成都双流国际机场，请您坐好并系好安全带，收起小桌板，调直座椅靠背，转机的乘客请先去海关办理申报手续，然后到国内航站楼候机，国内航站楼在国际航站楼旁边。谢谢。

2. Ladies and gentlemen,

女士们，先生们：

Our plane has landed at Shanghai Pudong International Airport. The local time is four o'clock. For your safety, please stay in your seat. Please use caution when taking items out from the overhead compartment. Your checked baggage may be claimed in the baggage claim area. The transit passengers please go to the connection flight counter in the arrival hall to complete the transfer formalities. Thank you for choosing Air China, and we wish you a nice day.

我们的飞机已经降落在上海浦东国际机场。当地时间是 4 点。为了您的安全，请您留在座位上。从头顶隔间取出物品时，请小心。您的托运行李可以在行李领取处领取，过境旅客请到下机旅客休息厅的转机柜台办理转机手续。

谢谢您选择中国航空公司，我们祝您旅途愉快。

Part IV Words and Expressions

1. belonging /bɪˈlɒŋɪŋ/ *n.* 附属品；附件

2. collect /kəˈlekt/ *vt.* 收集；收藏

3. continue /kənˈtɪnjuː/ *vi.* 持续；逗留

4. disembark /ˌdɪsɪmˈbɑːk/ *vt.& vi.* （使）登陆，登机

5. sincerely /sɪnˈsɪəli/ *adv.* 真诚地

6. apologize /əˈpɒlədʒaɪz/ *vi.* 道歉，认错

7. procedure /prəˈsiːdʒə(r)/ *n.* 程序

8. schedule /ˈʃedjuːl/ *n.* 手续计划

9. transfer /trænsˈfɜː(r)，ˈtrænsfɜː(r)/ *v.* 日程转移；换乘

Part V   Reading Skill

得体的语言
Proper Language

在客舱服务中，迎接、问候乘客，回答乘客提出的问题或向乘客进行说服工作时，都需要沟通。这时得体的语言就显得尤为重要。在客舱服务中，对乘客的称呼体现了乘务员的服务态度，也反映了对乘客的关注程度。称呼不当，会引起乘客的不满，甚至产生反感，从而影响沟通效果，降低服务质量。服务时，一般称男士为"先生"，称未婚的年轻女性为"小姐"，称已婚女性为"太太"，无法确定该女性乘客是否已婚时，称其"女士"。

Part VI   Practical Practice

1. Match the expressions in Column A with their Chinese equivalents in Column B.

Column A	Column B
(1) declare	a. 申报
(2) procedure	b. 换乘
(3) transfer	c. 国内的
(4) domestic	d. 递送
(5) delivery	e. 程序

2. Translate the following sentences into English.

（1）收起小桌板，调直座椅靠背。

（2）您的托运行李可以在行李领取处领取。

3. Translate the following sentences into Chinese.

(1) If you have a connecting flight, you'll have to go to the domestic terminal after you have declared Customs.

(2) The transit passengers, please go to the connection flight counter in the arrival hall to complete the transfer formalities.

4. Practice oral English.

(1) Ladies and gentlemen,

We regret to announce that mechanical trouble has made it necessary for us to transfer to another aircraft. Please disembark with all of your personal belongings and follow our ground staff. We apologize for the inconvenience caused.

Thank you for your kind understanding and cooperation!

(2) Ladies and gentlemen,

Our captain has advised that due to congestion at the airport/ airport staff striking/ unfavorable weather condition/ strong headwind/ air traffic control, we are unable to land at the moment. Our aircraft is expected to land in about 20 minutes. We shall keep you updated with any further information as we receive it.

Passengers planning to transfer at/ in _____ Airport, please contact our ground staff after landing to make necessary arrangements for you. They will help you with your connecting flight. If you require any further assistance, we will be glad to help you.

We apologize for the inconvenience and thank you for your understanding.

Task 16
Stopover Flight Reminder

Less is more.
简单就是美。

Learning Objectives
Knowledge Objectives 1. To know how to make an announcement about stopover flight reminder 2. To learn some useful expressions about stopover flight reminder **Skill Objectives** 1. To be able to master the key words and expressions 2. To be able to know liaison rule **Quality Objectives** 1. To develop the sense of customer first and standardized service 2. To be knowledgeable and professional

Part I Lead-in

Question:

(1) Do you know what stopover flight is?

(2) Which airlines offer a stopover?

(3) How to book free stopovers online?

Part II Background Information

飞机之所以经停，主要的原因有飞机没油了需要进行加油或者飞机存在问题需要进行及时检查。如果飞机机舱并没有坐满乘客，经停的目的是载客，提高飞机的上座率。一般来说，飞机的经停时间比较短，大家不要轻易下飞机。最多经停时间是 30 分钟，大家可以在登机口休息片刻，但是不要跟随出站旅客一起离开而造成误机。飞机航班中转的情况也可以被称为"中转联程"，其实大家可以直接将其理解为与火车联程票是一样的。只是旅客选择中转再到达目的地而已，因为中转联程的机票价格比正常直达航班票价优惠很多，所以它很受旅客的青睐，也是自费出行的首选。

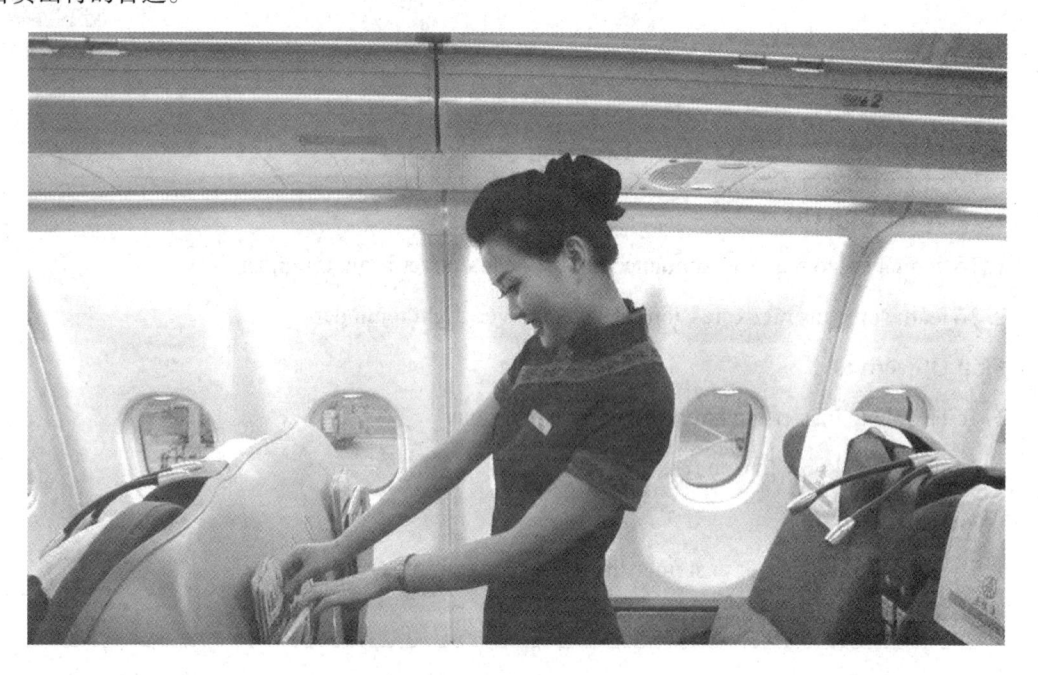

Part III Let's Read

Ladies and gentlemen,

　　We have just landed at airport; the time now is_____. The airport is _____kilometers away from downtown. Our plane is still taxiing. Please keep your seat belts fastened and make sure your mobile phones are off until the "Fasten Seat Belt" sign has been turned off.

　　For passengers arriving at this airport, please take all your belongings and get your boarding pass ready for the check by ground staff. Please collect your check-in luggage at the luggage claim area.

（旅客携带全部行李物品下机）For passengers continuing on to_____. Please disembark with all your hand luggage and take note of the boarding announcement while resting at the waiting hall. Items not claimed will be removed from the plane. （旅客只带贵重/大件物品）For passengers continuing on to_____, You need to disembark, the ground staff will guide you to the waiting hall. Please take your valuables and boarding pass with you. Your hand luggage may be left on board. If you want to terminate your trip in_____, please tell us before disembark.

（旅客不下机）Passengers continuing on to_____, please wait on board. We will stay here for a short while. Lavatories can be used, however smoking is not allowed.

(We sincerely apologize again for the delay of this flight.)

Thank you for flying with Dong Hai Airlines. See you next time and have a nice day!

女士们，先生们：

我们已经在机场着陆，现在时间是_____，机场距离市区_____千米。

飞机还将继续滑行，在安全带信号灯熄灭前，请坐在座位上并且关闭手机。

到达机场的旅客，请带好您的全部手提物品先下飞机，下机时请准备好您的登机牌，以便地面服务人员核查。您的交运行李请在行李提取处领取。

（旅客携带全部行李物品下机）继续前往_____的旅客请您携带全部个人行李物品下飞机，在候机楼休息时请注意广播通知再次登机。遗留在客舱中的物品，将会被卸下飞机。

（旅客只带贵重/大件物品）继续前往_____的旅客，您也需要下飞机，地勤人员将会指导您去候机厅。手提物品可以放在飞机上，请您随身携带贵重物品和登机牌。如果您需要终止航程，不再继续前往_____，请务必在下机前告知乘务员，我们将协助您办理相关手续。

（旅客不下机）：继续前往_____的旅客，您不需要下飞机。我们的飞机在这里只做短暂停留，机上等待期间请您不要吸烟，洗手间可以正常使用。

（对于本次航班的延误，我们再次向您深表歉意）。

感谢您搭乘东海航空公司的班机。祝您旅途愉快，期望下次旅途再会！

Part IV Words and Expressions

1. belonging /bɪˈlɒŋɪŋ/ *n.* 附属品；附件

2. collect /kəˈlekt/ *v.* 收集；收藏

3. continue /kənˈtɪnjuː/ *v.* 持续；逗留

4. disembark /ˌdɪsɪmˈbɑːk/ *v.* （使）登陆，登机

5. sincerely /sɪnˈsɪəli/ *adv.* 真诚地

6. apologize /əˈpɒlədʒaɪz/ *v.* 道歉，认错

Part V   Reading Skill

缩读

Liaison Rule

在快速的语流节奏中，英语中有些词的连接会产生明显的缩读，例如，gonna, wanna, gotta 的口语缩读法：

be going to 缩读的形式为 be gonna；

want to 缩读的形式为 wanna；

got to 缩读的形式为 gotta；

kind of 缩读的形式为 kinda；等等。

be gonna /ˈɡɔnə/：be going to 将要，打算；

wanna /ˈwɔnə/：want to 想要；

('ve/'s) gotta /ˈɡɔtə/：have/has got to 不得不，得（'ve/'s 常被省略）。

Part VI   Practical Practice

1. Match the expressions in Column A with their Chinese equivalents in Column B.

Column A   Column B

(1) belongings   a. 真诚地

(2) sincerely   b. 随身物品

(3) continue   c. 逗留

(4) disembark   d. 道歉

(5) apologize   e. 登机

2. Translate the following sentences into English.

（1）到达此机场的旅客，请带好您的全部手提物品先下飞机，下机时请准备好您的登机牌，以便地面服务人员核查。

(2) 对于本次航班的延误，我们向您深表歉意。

3. Translate the following sentences into Chinese.

(1) Please disembark with all your hand luggage and take note of the boarding announcement while resting at the waiting hall.

(2) Our plane is still taxiing. Please keep your seat belts fastened and make sure your mobile phone is off until the "Fasten Seat Belt" sign has been turned off.

4. Practice oral English.

Ladies and gentlemen,

We are sorry to inform you that we are heading direct to _____ Airport due to unfavorable weather conditions at _____ Airport (airport has been closed). We expect to land at_____ Airport at about _____ a.m./ p.m. We apologize for the inconvenience.

Thank you for your cooperation!

Task 17
Level Flight

Deliberate in counsel, prompt in action.
考虑要仔细，行动要迅速。

微课抢先看

Learning Objectives
Knowledge Objectives
1. To know how to make an announcement of level flight
2. To learn some useful expressions about flight safety check
Skill Objectives
1. To be able to master the key words and expressions
2. To be able to know the reading skill of oral control exercises
Quality Objectives
1. To develop the sense of responsibility
2. To be knowledgeable and professional

Part I   Lead-in

Question:

(1) Do you know what level flight is?

(2) What is the difference between altitude and flight level?

(3) What is straight and level flight in aviation?

(4) How do you calculate the altitude of a plane?

Part II Background Information

伴随着发动机隆隆的轰鸣声，飞机开始滑行、加速，直至腾空而起，经过爬升终于来到平飞高度。水平飞行简称"平飞"，是指保持一定高度的飞行，如水平定常直线飞行，水平直线加、减速飞行，水平面内的机动飞行等。定常飞行是指无加速度的飞行；水平直线飞行是指飞机在水平面内保持直线航迹的飞行。

Part III Let's Read

1. 平飞广播

Notice: For economy cabin only.

Ladies and gentlemen:

Our aircraft has left. We will provide you with a beverage and (breakfast/lunch/dinner/refreshment/snack) service shortly.

(Breakfast/Lunch/Dinner/Refreshment) is about to be offered after _____hours_____minutes prior to landing. And the duty free sales will begin after the meal.

Please keep your seat belts fastened when seated in case of sudden turbulence. Once again, all mobile phones need to be powered off during entire flight. While using your personal laptop, please make sure the WiFi function has been switched off. We will be by your side any time you need anything from us. We wish you a pleasant trip.

注意：只限经济舱。

女士们，先生们：

飞机已进入平飞状态。我们正在为您准备早餐/午餐/晚餐/点心以及饮料，稍后您就可以享用了。我们将在着陆前_____小时_____分为您提供早餐/午餐/晚餐/便餐。餐后，我们还将售卖免税商品。

为了防止意外颠簸，就座时请系好安全带。再次提醒您，旅途中请不要打开手机。在您使用个人电脑时，请记得关闭无线网卡功能。如您需要服务，请随时告诉我们。祝您旅途愉快。

2. 平飞广播

Notice: For economy cabin only.

Ladies and gentlemen:

Our aircraft has left. We will provide you with a beverage and breakfast/lunch/dinner/refreshment/snack service shortly.

Please keep your seat belts fastened when seated in case of sudden turbulence. Once again, portable power banks and mobile phones, even in flight mode, are not permitted during the entire flight. While using your personal laptop, please make sure the WiFi function has been switched off. We will be by your side any time you need anything from us. We wish you a pleasant trip.

注意：仅限经济舱。

女士们，先生们：

飞机已进入平飞状态。我们正在为您准备早餐/午餐/晚餐/点心/饮料，稍后您就可以享用了。

为了防止意外颠簸，就座时请系好安全带。再次提醒您，旅途中请不要打开包括带有"飞行模式"功能的手机，不要使用充电宝或给充电宝充电。在您使用电脑时，请记得关闭无线网卡功能。如果您需要服务，请随时告诉我们。祝您旅途愉快。

3. 夜间飞行广播

Ladies and gentlemen,

To ensure a good rest, we will dim the cabin lights. If you would like to read, you may use the reading light over your head. As a precaution against sudden turbulence, we advise you to keep your seat belt fastened while seated. Please press the call button for service.

Thank you.

女士们，先生们：

为了使您在旅途中得到良好的休息，我们将调暗客舱灯光，需要阅读书刊的旅客，可以打开您头顶上方的阅读灯。为预防突发颠簸，请您系好安全带。如您需要帮助，请按呼叫铃。谢谢。

Part IV   Words and Expressions

1. provide sth for sb 提供东西给某人

    provide sb with sth 提供某人东西

2. beverage /ˈbɛvərɪdʒ/ *n.* 饮料

3. refreshment /riˈfrɛʃmənt/ *n.* 点心；起提神作用的东西

4. snack /snæk/ *n.* 小吃；快餐 late snack 宵夜；夜餐

5. in case of 万一；如果发生；假设

6. portable /ˈpotəbl/ *adj.* 便携的；可饮用的

7. function /ˈfʌŋkʃən/ *n.* 功能

8. ensure /ɪnˈʃʊr/ *v.* 确保，保证

9. precaution /prɪˈkɔːʃ(ə)n/ *n.* 预防；警惕

10. turbulence /ˈtɜːbjʊl(ə)ns/ *n.* 湍流

Part V   Reading Skill

口腔控制练习

<center>Oral Control Exercises</center>

口腔控制练习要求字正腔圆，发音圆融饱满。

（1）发音时，颧肌提起，像兴奋地要唱歌或者笑的感觉。此时口腔前上部有展宽感，鼻孔也随之张大，嘴唇也呈现微笑状。

（2）牙关打开，才能使舌头活动范围增大，这样才更有利于字音的清晰表达，也给声音增加了明亮、刚劲的色彩。

（3）软腭挺起，即软腭部分向上用力，这个动作可以使口腔后部空间加大，并减少灌入鼻腔的气流，避免过多的鼻音色彩。挺软腭可以用"半打哈欠"或"举杯痛饮"的动作来体会。

（4）在吐字发音的过程中，下巴向内微收，处于放松、从动的状态，不能着意，更不能着力。

Part VI   Practical Practice

1. Match the expressions in Column A with their Chinese equivalents in Column B.

Column A   Column B

(1) snack   a. 确保

(2) ensure   b. 颠簸

(3) turbulence   c. 小吃

(4) precaution   d. 预防

(5) portable   e. 便携的

2. Translate the following sentences into English.

（1）为了防止意外颠簸，就座时请系好安全带。

（2）我们正在为您准备早餐与小吃。

3. Translate the following sentences into Chinese.

(1) Once again, all mobile phones need to be powered off during entire flight.

(2) As a precaution against sudden turbulence, we advise you to keep your seat belt fastened while seated.

4. Practice oral English.

(1) Ladies and gentlemen,

To ensure a good rest during this trip, we will dim the cabin lights. If you would like to read, please switch on your reading light located over your head.

Please fasten your seatbelt while you are seated and use the call button if you need any assistance.

Thank you.

(2) Ladies and gentlemen,

This is your purser speaking. Welcome aboard _____ Airlines.

The plane you are taking is Airbus 320. Now we are going to _____, the whole flight takes about _____ hours _____ minutes. We will be landing at our destination at _____(time). This is our golden flight. According to the regulation of CAAC, to be safe, we will provide cabin service after take-off 20 minutes. Today we have prepared lunch and several beverages.

We have prepared some nice items for you. Please enjoy your shopping time later. For your convenience of travel, you can get the application forms of _____ club and comment card from our cabin crew.

We may encounter some turbulence, please fasten your seatbelt when you are seated. And make the seatbelt outside your blanket to avoid being bothered.

We wish you a pleasant journey!

Thank you!

Task 18
Declaration Card

Don't put off for tomorrow what you can do today.
今日事今日毕。

Learning Objectives
Knowledge Objectives
1. To know how to make an announcement about declaration card
2. To learn some useful words and expressions
Skill Objectives
1. To be able to master the key words and expressions
2. To be able to learn reading skill of reappearance of scene
Quality Objectives
1. To develop the awareness of professional standards and professional norms
2. To be knowledgeable and professional

Part I Lead-in

Question:

(1) What preparations should one make if he wants to visit Australia?

(2) What is the function of green and red lanes?

(3) Can you list some of the prohibited items?

Part II Background Information

乘客出入境一般要办理以下 4 种检查手续：边防检查、海关检查、安全检查、卫生检疫。然而，不同的国家检查的内容及所办手续有很大的不同。

世界上各国普遍都设立海关，对出入境人员携带的货物进行检查，哪些可以免税、哪些需要征税，都有明确的规定。因此，乘客需选择"绿色"或"红色"通道，填写携带物品入境申报单。通常烟、酒等物品按限额放行；文物、武器、毒品、动植物等为违禁品。边防检查时主要检查出入境登记卡，有时登记卡在飞机上由航空公司代发，可提前填写，入境时校验护照、检查签证等（有些国家不要求填写入境卡片）即可。出境时，许多国家还需填写卡片，并将其连同护照和登机牌交给工作人员检查。

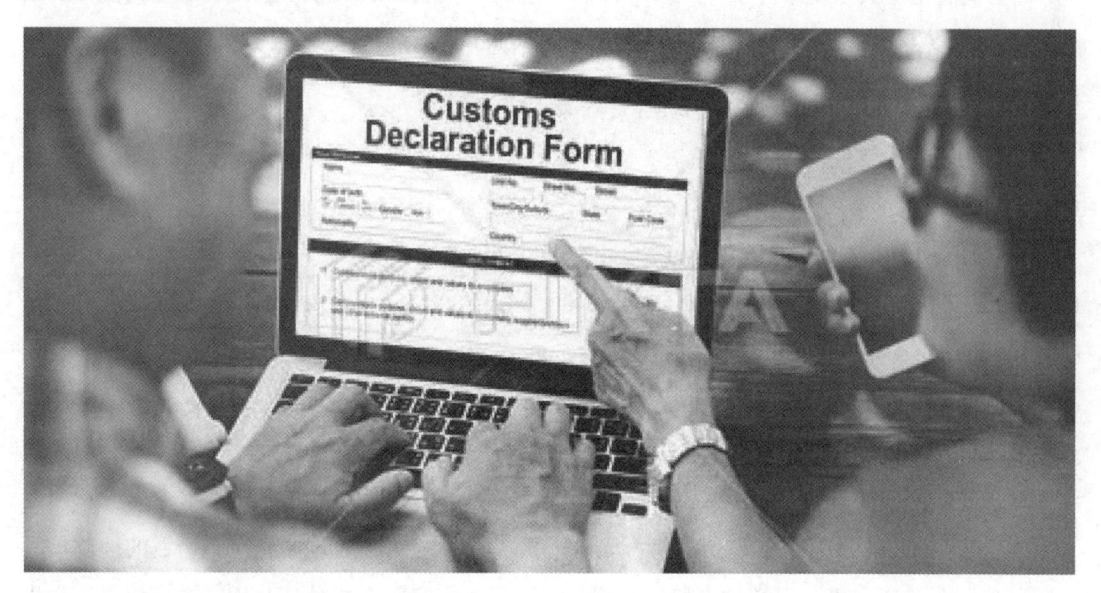

Part III Let's Read

1. 申报单和入境卡

Ladies and gentlemen,

In order to speed up your arrival formalities at _____ Airport, all passengers, including minors (who are not local citizens), are advised to complete all entry forms for Customs, Immigration and Quarantine before landing. If you have any questions, please contact the flight attendant. Thank you!

女士们，先生们：

为了在_____机场加快办理抵达手续，除当地公民外，所有旅客包括未成年人在着陆前都要填写入境卡。落地后交予海关和移民局工作人员。如需要帮助，请与乘务员联系，谢谢！

2. 发放 CIQ 单据

Ladies and gentlemen,

We will be distributing the Arrival Card / Immigration Card/ Customs Declaration Form/ Health Declaration Form. If you have any problems filling in the form, please feel free to contact us and we will be glad to help you. After landing, please hand the completed forms to the officials of the Customs and Immigration Authority. Thank you!

女士们，先生们：

现在我们将发放入境卡/移民卡/海关申报单/健康申报表。如果您在填写时有任何问题，请随时告诉我们，我们非常乐意协助您。落地后，请将填好的表格交给海关和移民局工作人员。谢谢！

3. 填写海关、移民和检疫表格

Ladies and gentlemen,

May I have your attention please? In order to speed up arrival formalities in Los Angeles International Airport, you are advised to fill in the forms for Customs, Immigration and Quarantine before reaching your destination. All forms are supposed to be filled out in English. All members of one family please use one Declaration Form. If you have any problems, please ask our flight attendants.

女士们，先生们：

大家请注意。为了加快办理到达洛杉矶国际机场的手续，我们建议您在到达目的地前填写海关、移民和检疫表格。所有的表格都要用英文填写。家庭所有成员请使用一张申报表。如果您有什么问题，请咨询空乘人员。

Part IV Words and Expressions

1. immigration /ˌɪmɪˈgreɪʃn/ *n.* 移民
2. quarantine /ˈkwɒrəntiːn/ *n.* 检疫
3. Arrival/Departure Record Form 出入境登记表
4. Customs Declaration Form 海关申报表

5. Customs and Immigration Authority 海关和移民局

6. formality /fɔːˈmæləti/ n. 正式手续；仪式

7. entry /ˈentri/ n. 进入（许可）

   entry forms 入境表格

8. export /ɪkˈspɔːt, ˈekspɔːt/ v. 出口；出境

9. import /ˈɪmpɔːt, ɪmˈpɔːt/ v. 进口；入境

10. fill /fɪl/ v. 装满；占满

    fill in the form 填写表格

Part V Reading Skill

情景再现

Reappearance of Scene

在符合稿件需要的前提下，以稿件提供的材料为原型，使稿件中的人物、事件、情节、场面、景物、情绪等在播音员脑海里不断浮现，形成连续活动的画面，并不断引发相应的态度、感情，这个过程就是情景再现。

（1）理清头绪。我们头脑里连续的活动画面开头是什么？接下来是怎么变化的？以后又怎样发展？结果是怎样的？哪里是重点的特写镜头？

（2）设身处地。设身处地主要是为了获得现场感，产生"我就在"的感觉。

（3）触景生情。在毫无准备的情况下，一个具体的"景"的刺激，马上引起我们具体的"情"，而又完全符合稿件的要求。

Part VI Practical Practice

1. Match the expressions in Column A with their Chinese equivalents in Column B.

   Column A   Column B
   (1) immigration   a. 出口
   (2) quarantine   b. 手续
   (3) formality   c. 海关
   (4) export   d. 移民
   (5) Customs   e. 检疫

2. Translate the following sentences into English.

（1）现在我们将发放入境卡/海关申报单/健康申报表。

（2）所有的表格都要用英文填写。

3. Translate the following sentences into Chinese.

(1) If you have any problems filling in the form, please feel free to contact us and we will be glad to help you.

(2) All members of one family please use one Declaration Form.

4. Practice oral English.

Ladies and gentlemen,

We will be distributing the Arrival Card / Immigration Card/ Customs Declaration Form/ Health Declaration Form. If you have any problems filling in the form, please feel free to contact us and we will be glad to help you.

After landing, please hand the completed forms to the officials of the Customs and Immigration Authority.

Thank you.

Task 19

Shopping

The eye is bigger than the belly.

贪多嚼不烂。

Learning Objectives
Knowledge Objectives
1. To know how to make an announcement about shopping
2. To learn some useful expressions about shopping in the cabin
Skill Objectives
1. To be able to master the key words and expressions about shopping
2. To be able to know the reading skill of the pause
Quality Objectives
1. To develop the sense of serious and enthusiastic service
2. To be knowledgeable and professional

Part I Lead-in

Question:

(1) How to buy duty-free items?

(2) How to give passengers suggestions on duty-free shopping?

Part II Background Information

在提供机上免税购物服务的时候，各个航空公司大致都有以下的流程：首先，乘务员播报机上免税购物的广播词；其次，乘客翻阅前方座椅口袋中的免税购物杂志；最后，乘务员推着小购物车穿过机舱过道来展示免税商品，这时，乘客就可以购买自己心仪的商品了。

在机场国际航班休息区、过境转机大厅和国际航班上都可以购买免税商品。在国际航班上，乘务员会销售机上免税购物杂志上所展示的商品。因为免税商品免除了关税，所以价格一般要比零售价格便宜 15%~40%。免税商品一般都是全球知名品牌的商品，包括化妆品、珠宝首饰、配饰、糕点、糖果、酒水、儿童玩具等。

Part III Let's Read

1. Ladies and gentlemen,

In an effort to further meet your traveling needs, we are pleased to offer you a wide selection of duty-free items. All items are priced in US dollars. Please check with your cabin attendant for prices in other currencies. Most major currencies and US dollar travelers' checks are accepted for your purchases. The major credit cards are also accepted. Detailed information can be found in the Duty-free Catalog in the seat pocket in front of you.

女士们，先生们：

为了进一步满足您的旅行需求，我们很高兴为您提供种类丰富的免税商品。所有商品均以美元计价。请向乘务员查询其他货币的价格。绝大多数通用货币和美元旅行支票均可支付，也可使用信用卡。更多免税品目录的详细资料放置在您座位前方口袋中。

2. Ladies and gentlemen,

Good morning!

Continental Airlines introduces another special service for you on this flight: a unique shopping experience while flying. Within the pages of the newest Continental Collection, you will discover an unparalleled collection to of over 60 items from the world's most sought after names: jewelry from Misaki, Carolee and Swarovski, watches from Anne Klein and Kenneth Cole, toys, liquor, fragrances and cosmetics, all available to purchase duty-free while on board and to take with you.

Look for a copy of the Continental Collection catalog in the seat pocket on board. Your flight attendant will be pleased to assist you with your selection.

All prices are in U.S. dollars. Most major currencies, traveler's checks and credit cards are accepted.

Enjoy your shopping and fight.

Thank you!

女士们，先生们：

早上好！

美国大陆航空公司为您介绍另一种特殊服务：独特的飞行购物体验。最新物品的页面中有世界上最受欢迎的60多件物品的名字。例如，米萨基的珠宝，卡罗琳和施华洛世奇，安妮克莱因和肯尼斯科尔的手表、玩具、酒、香水和化妆品，都可以免税购买并随身携带。在客舱的座位前排座椅下方口袋里有商品目录。我们非常愿意协助您进行挑选。

所有价格按美元结算。绝大多数通用货币、旅行支票和信用卡都可支付。

祝您旅途及购物愉快，谢谢！

Part IV Words and Expressions

1. duty /ˈdjuːtiˈ/ *n.* 责任；关税

    duty-free item 免税商品

    duty-free shopping 免税购物

duty-free catalog 免税商品目录

duty-free allowance 免税限额

2. selection /siˈlekʃ(ə)n/ n. 选择

3. purchase /ˈpɜrtʃəs/ n. 购买，采购

4. cash /kæʃ/ n. 现金

5. credit card 信用卡

6. unparalleled /ʌnˈpærəleid/ adj. 无与伦比的；独特的

7. brand /brænd/ n. 品牌

8. jewelry /ˈdjuːəlri/ n. 珠宝

9. liquor /ˈlikər/ n. 酒；含酒精的饮料

10. fragrance /ˈfreigrəns/ n. 香水

11. perfume /ˈpɜfjum/ n. 香水；香味

12. cosmetic /kʌzˈmetik/ n. 化妆品

13. accessory /əkˈsesəri/ n. 配饰；配件

14. confectionery /kənˈfekʃəneri/ n. 糕点

15. cigarette /sigˈreit/ n. 香烟

16. whiskey /ˈwiski/ n. 威士忌

Part V　Reading Skill

停顿

Read the Pause

朗读时，有些句子较短，按书面标点停顿就可以。有些句子较长，结构较复杂，句中虽然没有标点符号，但为了表达清楚意思，中途也可以短暂地停顿。然而，如果停顿不当就会破坏句子的结构，这就叫读破句。朗读测试中忌读破句。正确的停顿有以下3种类型：

（1）标点符号停顿。标点符号是书面语言的停顿符号，也是朗读作品时语言停顿的重要依据。标点符号的停顿规律一般是：句号、问号、感叹号、省略号的停顿时间略长于分号、破折号、连接号；分号、破折号、连接号的停顿时间又长于逗号、冒号；逗号、冒号的停顿时间又长于顿号、间隔号。另外，在作品的段落之间，停顿的时间要比一般的句号时间长些。以上停顿，也不是绝对的。有时为表达感情的需要，在没有标点的地方也可以停顿，在有标点的地方也可以不停顿。

（2）语法停顿。语法停顿是句子中间的自然停顿。它往往是为了强调句子中主语、谓语、

宾语、定语、状语或补语而做的短暂停顿。学习语法有助于我们在朗读中正确地停顿断句，不读破句，正确地表达作品的思想内容。

（3）感情停顿。感情停顿不受书面标点和句子语法关系的制约，完全根据感情或心理的需要而进行停顿处理，它受感情支配，根据感情的需要决定停与不停。它的特点是声断而情不断，也就是声断情连。

Part VI   Practical Practice

1. Match the expressions in Column A with their Chinese equivalents in Column B.

Column A   Column B
(1) selection   a. 品牌
(2) brand   b. 酒
(3) liquor   c. 香水
(4) perfume   d. 选择
(5) cigarette   e. 香烟

2. Translate the following sentences into English.

（1）请向乘务员查询其他货币的价格。

（2）乘务员将很乐意协助您进行挑选。

3. Translate the following sentences into Chinese.

(1) Look for a copy of the Continental Collection catalog in the seat pocket on board.

(2) In an effort to further meet your traveling needs, we are pleased to offer you a wide selection of duty-free items.

4. Practice oral English.

Ladies and gentlemen,

For passengers interested in purchasing duty-free items, we have a wide selection for sale on this flight. All items are priced in U.S. dollars. Please check with the flight attendant for prices in other currencies. Detailed information can be found in the Duty-free Catalog in the seat pocket in front of you.

Thank you!

Task 20

Meals

Truth never grows old.
真理永存。

微课抢先看

Learning Objectives
Knowledge Objectives
1. To know how to make an announcement about meals
2. To learn some useful words and expressions
Skill Objectives
1. To be able to master the key words and expressions about meals
2. To be able to know reading skill of sense group
Quality Objectives
1. To develop the awareness of the sincerity and enthusiasm
2. To be knowledgeable and professional

Part I Lead-in

Question:

(1) Generally, do you know what the main dish is on board?

(2) When passengers are offered meals on board, beside the main dish, what else can they be served?

(3) What is the difference between the meal service of First Class and Economy Class?

Part II Background Information

在航空服务中，餐食服务是服务环节中的重点，有不同的航线时间的航班就提供不同的餐食选择。短程航线（1小时30分钟之内）的航班提供小吃、点心和矿泉水，其他航线航班根据实际情况提供早、午、晚餐服务。头等舱、商务舱和经济舱的餐食服务步骤和要求不同。头等舱和商务舱为点餐制，经济舱为发餐制，餐食组成一般有沙拉（开胃菜）、面包、水果、酸奶、热餐等，并且有饮料服务。各个航空公司除了将常规的餐食供应给乘客，还会根据乘客不同的身体需要、宗教习俗等提供特殊餐食。特殊餐食需要在乘客购票时或航班起飞前24小时向航空公司提出申请才得以在航班上配备，在航班中无法临时提供。申请了特殊餐食的乘客的信息会出现在乘客名单中，包括姓名、座位号、特殊餐食要求，航班起飞前的检查由乘务员负责，确保特殊餐食已经配备好。在餐食服务开始时，特殊餐食的发放应先完成。

Part III Let's Read

1. 供餐广播

Ladies and gentlemen,

In a few moments, the flight attendants will be serving meal/snacks and beverages. We hope you will enjoy them. For the convenience of the passenger seated behind you, please return your seat back to the upright position during our meal service. If you need any assistance, please feel comfortable to contact us. Thank you!

女士们，先生们：

我们将在几分钟后为您提供餐食/点心及各种饮料，希望您能喜欢。在用餐期间，请调直座椅靠背，以方便后排的旅客。如果您需要帮助，我们乐意为您服务。谢谢！

2. 膳食服务

Ladies and gentlemen,

We will soon be serving breakfast/lunch/dinner. We are offering you a choice of bread and noodles. We have also prepared a Muslim and a vegetarian meal. If you have special die requirements, please tell the flight attendants. Thank you!

女士们，先生们：

我们马上为您提供早餐/午餐/晚餐。我们为您准备了面包和面条可供您选择。我们还为您准备了清真餐和素食。如果您有特殊要求，请告知乘务员。谢谢！

3. 长期飞行服务广播

Ladies and gentlemen,

Meal will be served soon. We have a selection of chicken with rice and beef with noodles today. Welcome to make your choice. Please put down the table in front of you while we are serving you the meal. For the convenience of the passenger behind you, please return your seatback to the upright position during the meal service. Thank you!

女士们，先生们：

稍后将为您提供餐食。我们有鸡肉米饭和牛肉面条，欢迎选择。在我们为您服务的时候，请放下小桌板。为了方便后排的旅客，请您在用餐时将座位调成竖直状态。谢谢！

Part IV   Words and Expressions

1. meal service 餐食服务
2. snack /snæk/ *n.* 快餐；小吃
3. flavor /ˈfleɪvə/ *n.* 口味
4. menu /ˈmenjuː/ *n.* 菜单
5. starter /ˈstɑːtə/ *n.* 头盘；开胃小吃
6. appetizer /ˈæpɪˌtaɪzə/ *n.* 开胃菜
7. main dish/ main course 主菜

8. dessert /dɪˈzɜ:t/ *n.* 甜点

9. short-haul flight 短途航班

10. long-haul fight 长途航班

11. VGML   vegetarian meal (non dairy & egg) 素餐

12. VLML   vegetarian meal (containing egg & dairy) 西式素餐

13. AVML   Asian vegetarian meal 亚洲素餐

14. IVGML   Indian vegetarian meal 印度素餐

15. RVML   raw vegetarian meal 生蔬菜餐

16. EPML   fruit platter meal 水果餐

17. BBML   baby meal (1-2 years) 婴儿餐

18. BLML   bland meal (light easily digested meal) 软食、清淡、低纤维素餐

19. CHML   child meal 儿童餐

20. DBML   diabetic meal 糖尿病餐

21. GFML   gluten free meal 无麸质，无谷类餐

22. HFML   high fiber meal 高纤维餐

23. LCML   low calorie meal 低热量餐

24. LFML   low fat meal 低胆固醇，低脂肪餐

25. LPML   low protein meal 低蛋白质餐

26. LSML   low sodium/ no salt 低钠/无盐餐

Part V Reading Skill

意群

Sense Group

相邻的两词在意义上必须密切相关，同属于一个意群。连读所构成的音节一般都不重读，只需顺其自然地一带而过，不可读得太重（连读符号：~）。当短语或从句之间按意群进行停顿时，意群与意群之间即使有两个相邻的辅音与元音出现，也不可连读。

Is~it a~hat or a cat?（hat 与 or 之间不可以连读。）

There~is~a good book in my desk.（book 与 in 之间不可以连读。）

Can you speak~English or French?（English 与 or 之间不可以连续。）

Shall we meet at~eight or ten tomorrow morning?（meet 与 at，eight 与 or 之间不可以连读。）

She opened the door and walked~in.（door 与 and 之间不可以连读。）

不过这也不是绝对的，很多连读规则都是选择性的，按其中一种方法连读即可。

Part VI Practical Practice

1. Match the expressions in Column A with their Chinese equivalents in Column B.

Column A	Column B
(1) snack	a. 小吃
(2) flavor	b. 菜单
(3) menu	c. 开胃菜
(4) appetizer	d. 口味
(5) dessert	e. 甜点

2. Translate the following sentences into English.

（1）我们将为您提供餐食及各种饮料。

（2）如需要帮助，我们乐意为您服务。

3. Translate the following sentences into Chinese.

(1) For the convenience of the passenger seated behind you, please return your seat back to the upright position during our meal service.

(2) We have a selection of chicken with rice and beef with noodles today.

4. Practice oral English.

Attention please. _____Flight _____ to _____will be delayed because of weather conditions at _____. A further announcement will be made no later than 10:30. In the meantime passengers are invited to take light refreshments with the compliments of the airlines at the buffet in this lounge.

Task 21
Beverages

Reading makes a full man.

读书使人完善。

微课抢先看

Learning Objectives
Knowledge Objectives 1. To know how to make an announcement about beverages 2. To learn some useful words and expressions **Skill Objectives** 1. To be able to master the words and expressions about beverages 2. To be able to know broadcast rhythm and master rhythm skills **Quality Objectives** 1. To develop the sense of responsibility and the awareness of the service 2. To be knowledgeable and professional

Part I Lead-in

Question:

(1) How do the cabin attendants tell the passengers what drinks are available?

(2) How do the cabin attendants serve the coffee to the passengers?

(3) If a passenger wants a glass of red wine which has run out, what would a cabin attendant say to the passenger?

Part II Background Information

人们在搭乘飞机的时候，通常会点饮料。与餐食相比，饮料的选择比较多，包括冷饮，茶、咖啡等热饮。在飞行期间，通过使用餐车，空乘人员为客人提供各种饮料和不同种类的膳食。各个航空公司机上供应的饮料都各有不同，但一般会分为不含酒精类（Non-alcoholic）饮料和含酒精（Alcoholic）饮料两大类。

（1）不含酒精饮料又称软饮料（Soft Drink），其主要原料是饮用水或矿泉水、果汁、蔬菜汁，或者植物的根、茎、叶、花和果实的提取液。按性质和饮用对象将其分为特种用途饮料、保健饮料、餐桌饮料和大众饮料 4 类。软饮料包括咖啡（Coffee）、茶（Tea）、果汁（Juice）、矿泉水（Mineral Water）、可乐（Coke）等。

（2）含酒精饮料则包括啤酒（Beer）、葡萄酒（Wine）、鸡尾酒（Cocktails）和其他酒类。

Part III Let's Read

1. 饮料服务说明

Ladies and gentlemen, we will be serving you tea, coffee, and other soft drinks. Welcome to make your choice. Please put down the table in front of you. For the convenience of the passenger behind you, please return your seat back to the upright position. Thank you!

女士们，先生们：

我们将为您提供茶、咖啡和其他软饮料，欢迎选择。请放下您前面的小桌板。为了方便您后面的旅客，请把您的座位调整到竖直的状态。

2. 不提供饮料服务声明

Ladies and gentlemen, we are sorry to inform you that we cannot serve you hot drinks on this flight because the water system is out of order. However, we will be able to serve cold drinks. We apologize for the inconvenience caused. Thank you for your understanding.

女士们，先生们：

我们很遗憾地通知您，因为热水系统出现了故障，我们不能在这次航班上为您提供热饮。不过，我们可以提供冷饮。对此造成的不便深表歉意。谢谢您的理解。

3. 出售饮料

Ladies and gentlemen, we will begin our beverage service shortly, followed by lunch (dinner). Whiskey and brandy are available for purchase in the main cabin. Thank you.

女士们，先生们：

稍后我们将为您提供饮料服务，然后是午餐（晚餐）。主客舱有威士忌和白兰地可供购买。谢谢。

Part IV　Words and Expressions

1. drink service　饮料服务
2. juice /dʒu:s/ *n.* 果汁；果肉
    apple juice　苹果汁
    orange juice　橙汁
    tomato juice　番茄汁
3. mineral /ˈmɪnərəl/ *n.* 矿物
    mineral water　矿泉水
4. carbonate /ˈkɑ:bəneɪt/ *n.* 碳酸盐
    carbonated water　气泡水
5. soda /ˈsəʊdə/ *n.* 苏打；碳酸钠
    soda water　苏打水
6. tonic /ˈtɒnɪk/ *n.* 滋补品；奎宁水
    tonic water　汤力水

7. soft drink 软饮料；不含酒精饮料

   Coca-Cola 可乐

   Pepsi 百事可乐

   Sprite 雪碧

   green tea 绿茶

8. alcoholic /ˌælkəˈhɒlɪk/ adj.（含）酒精的；饮酒引起的

   alcoholic beverage 含酒精饮料

9. ferment /fəˈment/ n. 酶；酵素

   fermented liquors 发酵酒精饮料

10. beer /bɪə(r)/ n. 啤酒

11. wine /waɪn/ n. 葡萄酒

    red wine 红葡萄酒

    white wine 白葡萄酒

Part V　Reading Skill

掌握好广播节奏技巧

Broadcast Rhythm Master Rhythm Skills

掌握好广播节奏技巧：

（1）有快慢之分。

（2）快慢交替进行。

（3）根据材料内容、情感，需要分清主导节奏和辅助节奏。

紧张型 vs. 轻快型；

高亢型 vs. 低沉型；

凝重型 vs. 舒缓型。

Part VI　Practical Practice

1. Match the expressions in Column A with their Chinese equivalents in Column B.

Column A　　　　　　　　　Column B

(1) mineral water　　　　　　a. 汤力水

(2) tonic water　　　　　　　b. 矿泉水

(3) alcoholic beverages   c. 龙舌兰酒

(4) beer   d. 啤酒

(5) tequila   e. 酒精饮料

2. Translate the following sentences into English.

（1）我们将为您提供茶、咖啡和其他软饮料。

（2）不过，我们可以提供冷饮。

3. Translate the following sentences into Chinese.

(1) We are sorry to inform you that we cannot serve you hot drinks on this flight because the water system is out of order.

(2) We apologize for the inconvenience caused.

4. Practice oral English.

Ladies and gentlemen,

  This is your purser speaking. Welcome aboard_____ Airlines.

  The plane you are taking is Airbus 320. Now we are going to Shanghai, the whole flight takes about 2 hours 15 minute. We will be landing at our destination at 14:35. This is our golden flight. According to regulation of CAAC, to be safe, we will provide cabin service after take-off 20 minutes. Today we have prepared lunch and several beverages.

  We have prepared some nice items for you, please enjoy your shopping time later. For your convenience of travel, you can get the application forms of Fortune Wings Club and comment card from our cabin crew.

  We may encounter some turbulence, please fasten your seat belt when you are seated and make the seat belt outside your blanket to avoid being bothered.

  We wish you a pleasant journey!

  Thank you!

Task 22
Ground Temperature

Time and tide wait for on man.
时不我待。

Learning Objectives
Knowledge Objectives 1. To know how to make an announcement about ground temperature 2. To learn some useful words and expressions **Skill Objectives** 1. To be able to master the key words and expressions about ground temperature 2. To be able to know the reading skill of the expression on temperature **Quality Objectives** 1. To develop the awareness of the sincerity and enthusiasm 2. To be knowledgeable and professional

Part I Lead-in

Question:

What would happen to the passengers if they feel uncomfortable due to temperature in the cabin?

Part II Background Information

关于空调温度的问题。实际上我们平时坐飞机的时候都会觉得机场里面的温度比较低。在夏天的时候，我们穿的衣服都是比较凉爽的，因此在座位上可能会感到瑟瑟发抖。事实上在飞机飞行的过程当中，空调温度是不能调高的。在飞行当中，因为机舱压力需要控制，飞机内会将空调温度降低，假如温度过高，可能会导致乘客出现晕厥。在这种情况下，你可以向空姐要毛毯，而不是要求空姐把空调温度升高。

Part III Let's Read

1. 空调制冷效果不佳的安抚广播

Ladies and gentlemen,

　　We are now waiting for the flight departure. You may feel a little bit hot now due to the air conditioning system doesn't work well before take-off. We regret for this inconvenience at the moment. You'll feel better after take-off. Thank you!

女士们，先生们：

　　我们现在正在等待起飞。由于本架飞机的空调制冷系统在起飞前不能正常工作，造成目前客舱温度偏高，给您带来不适，我们深表歉意，这种情况会在飞机起飞后很快缓解。谢谢！

Task 22 Ground Temperature

2. 客舱外温度提醒（时间：机组通知飞机落地后）

Ladies and gentlemen,

Our plane has landed at _____ airport. The local time is____. The temperature outside is ____ degrees Celsius, (degrees Fahrenheit.) The plane is taxiing. For your safety, please stay in your seat for the time being. When the aircraft stops completely and the Fasten Seat Belt sign is turned off, Please detach the seat belt, take all your carry-on items and disembark (please detach the seat belt and take all your carry-on items and passport to complete the entry formalities in the terminal). Please use caution when retrieving items from the overhead compartment. Your checked baggage may be claimed in the baggage claim area. The transit passengers please go to the connection flight counter in the waiting hall to complete the procedures. It is raining/snowing outside, please be careful while getting out of the plane.

女士们，先生们：

我们已抵达_____机场，当地时间是_____，机舱外温度是_____摄氏度（华氏_____）。

飞行还将滑行一段时间，出于安全考虑请您系好安全带。当飞机完全停下来，并且安全带指示灯熄灭，请解开安全带，带好随身物品，离开飞机（请解开安全带，携带随身物品和护照在航站楼完成入境手续）。下机时请小心打开行李架，以免行李滑落。请到候机楼行李提取处领取您的托运行李。需要转机的旅客请到候机厅的转机台办理手续。

外面正在下雨／雪，下机时请注意地面路滑。

Part IV Words and Expressions

1. Celsius /ˈselsiəs/ *n.* 摄氏度
2. Fahrenheit /ˈfærənhaɪt/ *adj.* 华氏温度计的
   degrees Fahrenheit 华氏的
3. disembark /ˌdɪsɪmˈbɑːk/ *v.* 离机
4. detach /dɪˈtætʃ/ *v.* 解开
5. entry /ˈentri/ *n.* 进入；入口
   entry formalities 入境手续
6. caution /ˈkɔːʃn/ *n.* 注意；小心
7. temperature /ˈtemprətʃə(r)/ *n.* 温度
   ground temperature 地面温度

surface temperature 地表温度

8. claim /kleɪm/ *v.* 声称；索取

baggage claim area 行李认领区

Part V Reading Skill

在英文中如何表达温度？

How to Express the Temperature in English?

例句：The ground temperature is __ degrees Celsius or __ degrees Fahrenheit.

____的地面温度____摄氏度，____华氏度。

在表示温度时，用 below zero 表示零下温度，温度表示用基数词+degree（s）+单位词（centigrade 摄氏或 Fahrenheit 华氏）表示。

thirty-six degrees Celsius 或 36℃。

four degrees below zero Celsius 或−4℃。

Water freezes at thirty-two degrees Fahrenheit. 水在华氏 32° 时结冰。

Water boils at one hundred degrees Celsius. 水在摄氏 100° 时沸腾。

在人们都很清楚这里的单位词是什么度量制度时，可以省略单位词。

You are 37℃.（读作 thirty-seven degrees。）你是 37℃。

It's seven degrees below zero. 今天是−7℃。

There is an hour time difference between____ and ____. The local time is ____ a.m./ p.m. on ____（date）. The ground temperature is ____ degrees Celsius or degrees Fahrenheit.

____与____的时差为 1 小时，现在是当地时间____日上午/下午/晚上____。温度____摄氏度（可以替换成华氏度）。

Part VI Practical Practice

1. Match the expressions in Column A with their Chinese equivalents in Column B.

Column A   Column B

(1) detach   a. 取回

(2) retrieving   b. 注意；小心

(3) Celsius   c. 摄氏度

(4) caution   d. 地面温度

(5) ground temperature　　　　　　　e. 解开

2. Translate the following sentences into English.

（1）为了您的安全，请在座位上耐心等候。

（2）外面的温度是 20 摄氏度。

3. Translate the following sentences into Chinese.

(1) When the aircraft stops completely and the Fasten Seat Belt sign is turned off, please detach the seat belt, take all your carry-on items and disembark.

(2) The transit passengers please go to the connection flight counter in the waiting hall to complete the procedures.

4. Practice oral English.

Ladies and gentlemen,

We are waiting clearance from air traffic control. We apologize that the air-conditioning is not working properly while the plane is still on the ground. It will be improved after take-off.

Thank you for your understanding and cooperation!

Task 23

Recreation

After rain comes fair weather.

否极泰来。

Learning Objectives
Knowledge Objectives 1. To know how to make an announcement of recreation 2. To learn some useful expressions about recreation **Skill Objectives** 1. To be able to master the key words and expressions about recreation 2. To know to read nouns plurals and verbs **Quality Objectives** 1. To develop the awareness of the sincerity and enthusiasm 2. To be knowledgeable and professional

Part I Lead-in

Question:

(1) What kinds of in-flight entertainment system do we have on board?

(2) How to introduce the in-flight entertainment system in the cabin to the passengers?

Task 23　Recreation

Part II　Background Information

无论是高端的干线航空公司还是低成本的中小型航空公司，它们都非常关注机上娱乐系统的科学配置，从而最大化地满足不同乘客的需求。在航空业竞争激烈的今天，如何推广以乘客需求及科技发展为导向的机上娱乐系统，已经成为目前航空公司的策略化竞争手段之一。1921年，第一次在飞机上播放了电影，由此开启了机上娱乐的概念。机上娱乐在当时的定义是指航空旅行中，在机舱内为乘客提供任何可能实现的娱乐手段。随着科技的不断发展，允许乘客在飞机起降过程中使用开启了"飞行模式"的电子设备，这也意味着飞机起降过程中需要完全关闭电子设备已经成为历史。未来乘客个人的电子设备将在飞行中发挥更大的作用，而机上WiFi的逐步推广，也使乘客获得了自由的网络体验。

Part III　Let's Read

Ladies and gentlemen,

For your convenience of travel, we have prepared in-flight entertainment equipment for you. When you finish using it, please put it into the seat pocket in front of you. We wish you a pleasant journey.

女士们，先生们：

为了给您的旅途生活带来方便，我们在机上为您配备了娱乐设备，在您使用完毕后，请放回到您前面的座椅口袋中。预祝您旅途愉快。

Ladies and gentlemen,

Welcome on board. To make your flight more enjoyable, this aircraft is equipped with WiFi service and mobile phone service. We will let you know when you can connect during the flight. Live TV sport plus news from CCTV, BBC and more are also available on our entertainment system, thank you. Switch on your Wi-Fi and connect it to the network. You can use your laptop once the seat belt sign is off. Thank you!

女士们，先生们：

欢迎登机。为了使您的飞行更愉快，这架飞机配备了无线上网服务和移动电话服务。在飞行期间，我们会告诉您何时可以接通。现场直播的体育节目，以及来自中央电视台、英国广播公司等的新闻节目也可以在我们的娱乐系统上收看，谢谢。请打开您的WiFi并将其连接到网络。一旦安全带标识关闭，请使用您的笔记本电脑。谢谢!

Part IV　Words and Expressions

1. entertainment /ˌentəˈteɪnmənt/ *n.* 娱乐；款待；招待

2. opera /ˈɒprə/ *n.* 歌剧；歌剧院

3. cinema /ˈsɪnəmə/ *n.* 电影院

4. movie theater　电影院

5. pleasant /ˈpleznt/ *adj.* 愉快的

6. equipment /ɪˈkwɪpmənt/ *n.* 设施；设备

7. connect /kəˈnekt/ *v.* 连接；联结

8. laptop /ˈlæptɒp/ *n.* 笔记本电脑；便携式电脑

Part V　Reading Skill

名词复数及动词单数第三人称的读法
Reading of Plural Nouns and Verbs

名词复数及动词单数第三人称的读法：

（1）以/s/、/z/、/ʃ/、/ʒ/、/tʃ/、/dʒ/结尾的单词在变复数或单数第三人称时加es，读作/ɪz/，例如，buses, mazes, washes, matches, bridges。

（2）除了以上音结尾，所有以清辅音结尾的单词在变复数或单数第三人称时加s，读作/s/，例如，books, hopes。

（3）其余所有以浊辅音或者元音结尾的单词在变复数或单数第三人称时加 s，读作/z/，例如，dogs, eyes。

（4）结尾是/t/音的单词在变复数或单数第三人称时，要将最后的/t/和/s/读作/ts/，例如，rests, lifts。

（5）结尾是/d/音的单词在变复数或单数第三人称时，要将最后的/d/和/z/读作/dz/，例如，pretends, holds, friends。

Part VI Practical Practice

1. Match the expressions in Column A with their Chinese equivalents in Column B.

Column A	Column B
(1) entertainment	a. 便携式电脑
(2) equipment	b. 令人愉快的
(3) journey	c. 设备
(4) laptop	d. 旅程
(5) enjoyable	e. 娱乐

2. Translate the following sentences into English.

（1）在飞行期间，我们会告诉你什么时候可以接通。

（2）当安全带指示灯关闭，您就可以使用笔记本电脑了。

3. Translate the following sentences into Chinese.

(1) For your convenience of travel, we have prepared in-flight entertainment equipment for you.

(2) Switch on your WiFi and connect it to the network.

4. Practice oral English.

(1) Ladies and gentlemen,

For your convenience of travel, we have prepared in-flight entertainment equipment for you. When you finish using it, please put it into the seat pocket in front of you. We wish you a pleasant journey.

(2) Ladies and gentlemen,

We are sorry that the video system is not available on this flight. We sincerely apologize for the inconvenience caused.

Thank you for your understanding!

Task 24
Turbulence

If you want knowledge, you must toil for it.
要想求知，就得吃苦。

Learning Objectives
Knowledge Objectives
1. To know how to make an announcement about turbulence
2. To learn some useful expressions about turbulence
Skill Objectives
1. To be able to get the key words and expressions
2. To be able to master the reading skill of the pronunciation of Chinese stress
Quality Objectives
1. To develop the sense of awareness and responsibility
2. To be knowledgeable and professional

Part I Lead-in

Question:

(1) Flight delay happens very constantly. If it happens, what shall we do after flight delay announcement?

(2) Do you know what the considerations are when our flight is in turbulence?

Part II Background Information

造成飞机在飞行时颠簸的因素有很多，如低空乱流扰动会使进场飞机抖动颠簸，高空大气湍流也会造成飞机颠簸。那么，什么是飞机颠簸？飞机颠簸指飞机在飞行中突然出现的忽上忽下、左右摇晃及机身震颤等现象。飞机颠簸主要是由于飞机飞入扰动气流区，扰动气流使作用在飞机上的空气动力和力矩失去平绝飞行高度，飞行速度和飞机姿态等发生突然变化而引起的。飞机颠簸强度与扰动气汤、飞行速度、翼载荷等有关，颠簸一般分为轻度颠簸、中度颠簸、重度颠簸三种。

Part III Let's Read

1. Slight turbulence 轻度颠簸

Ladies and gentlemen,

Our aircraft is experiencing some turbulence. Please be seated, fasten your seat belt. Do not use the lavatories. Please watch out while taking meals.

女士们，先生们：

我们的飞机有些颠簸，请您坐好，系好安全带。洗手间暂停使用。正在用餐的旅客，请当心餐饮烫伤或弄脏衣物。

2. Moderate Turbulence 中度颠簸

Ladies and gentlemen,

Our aircraft is now experiencing some moderate turbulence, and it will last for some time. The captain has informed us that we will pass through an area of rough air in 5 minutes, the moderate turbulence will last for ten minutes. please be seated, fasten your seatbelt. Do not use the lavatories. Please watch out while taking meals. Cabin service well be suspended for a moment.

Thank you.

女士们，先生们：

飞机正经历较中度颠簸并且会持续一段时间。机长通知大家，大约在 5 分钟后，飞机将经过一段气流不稳定区，会有持续的较中度颠簸。请您坐好，系好安全带。洗手间暂停使用。正在用餐的旅客，请当心餐饮弄脏衣物。暂停客舱服务，请您谅解。谢谢。

3. Severe Turbulence 重度颠簸

Ladies and gentlemen,

We have met some severe turbulence, please take your seat and fasten your seat belts. Do not use the lavatories.

Cabin crew return to your jump seat.

女士们，先生们：

飞机正经历强烈的颠簸，请您尽快就座，系好安全带。洗手间暂停使用。客舱乘务人员各就各位。

Part IV　Words and Expressions

1. turbulence /ˈtɜːbjələns/ *n.* 强气流；湍流；紊流

2. fasten /ˈfɑːsn/ *v.* （使两部分）系牢，扎牢，结牢，扣紧

3. suspend /səˈspend/ *v.* 暂停；中止

4. rough /rʌf/ *adj.* 恶劣的；有暴风雨的

5. slight /slaɪt/ *adj.* 轻微的；略微的

6. moderate /ˈmɒdərət, ˈmɒdəreɪt/ *adj.* 有节制的；稳健的；温和的；适度的

7. severe /sɪˈvɪə(r)/ *adj.* 极为恶劣的；十分严重的

8. lavatory /ˈlævətri/ *n.* 卫生间；洗手间；盥洗室

Part V   Reading Skill

汉语重音的读法

The Pronunciation of Chinese Stress

汉语中，重音是指那些在表情达意上起重要作用的字、词或短语在朗读时要加以强调的技巧。重音是通过声音的强调来突出意义的，能给色彩鲜明、形象生动的词增加分量。重音有以下3种情况：

（1）语法重音。语法重音是按语言习惯自然重读的音节。这些重读的音节大都是按照平时的语言规律确定的。一般来说，语法重音不带特别强调的色彩。

（2）强调重音。强调重音不受语法制约，它是根据语句所要表达的重点决定的，它受应试者的意愿制约，在句子中的位置上是不固定的。强调重音的作用在于揭示语言的内在含义。由于表达目的不同，强调重音就会落在不同的词语上，所揭示的含义就不相同，表达的效果也不一样。

（3）感情重音。感情重音可以使朗读的作品色彩丰富，充满生气，有较强的感染力。感情重音大部分出现在表现内心节奏强烈，情绪激动的情况。

Part VI   Practical Practice

1. Match the expressions in Column A with their Chinese equivalents in Column B.

Column A   Column B

(1) turbulence   a. 保持

(2) severe   b. 卫生间

(3) rough   c. 严重的

(4) lavatory   d. 强大的

(5) maintenance   e. 颠簸

2. Translate the following sentences into English.

（1）由于航路交通管制，目前我们暂时无法确定起飞时间。

（2）请大家在座位上休息等候，如果有进一步的消息，我们会尽快通知您。

3. Translate the following sentences into Chinese.

(1) Our aircraft is now experiencing some moderate turbulence.

(2) Please be seated, fasten your seat belt. Do not use the lavatories. Please watch out while taking meals.

4. Practice oral English.

Ladies and gentlemen,

May I have your attention please?

Any passenger who has found a smart phone—Huawei Mate 20 pro, please contact our flight attendant immediately. Meanwhile, other passengers who have seen the article please offer us relevant clues.

Thank you!

Task 25
Air Traffic Control

Practice makes perfect.
熟能生巧。

Learning Objectives
Knowledge Objectives
1. To know how to make an announcement of air traffic control
2. To learn some useful expressions about air traffic control
Skill Objectives
1. To be able to get to know the key words and expressions
2. To be able to get to know the reading rhythm division skills
Quality Objectives
1. To develop the sense of time management and responsibility
2. To be knowledgeable and professional

Part I Lead-in

Question:

Flight delay happens very constantly. If it happens, what shall we do after flight delay announcement?

Task 25 Air Traffic Control

Part II Background Information

在飞行航线的空域划分不同的管理空域，包括航路、飞行情报管理区、进近管理区、塔台管理区、等待空域管理区等，并按管理区不同使用不同的雷达设备。在管理空域内进行间隔划分，飞机间的水平和垂直方向间隔构成空中交通管理的基础。由导航设备、雷达系统、二次雷达、通信设备、地面控制中心组成空中交通管理系统，完成监视、识别、导引覆盖区域内的飞机。

Part III Let's Read

1. 由于航空管制导致的机上等候

Ladies and gentlemen,

　　Due to air traffic control, we haven't been informed about the time of departure yet. Please wait for a moment until we have further information for you. We will be serving food and beverages while we are waiting for departure. Thank you!

女士们，先生们：

　　由于航路交通管制，目前我们暂时无法确定起飞时间，请大家在座位上等候，如果有进一步的消息，我们会尽快通知您。在此期间，我们将在等待起飞期间为您提供餐饮服务。谢谢您的理解与配合！

2. 由于飞机故障导致的机上等候

Ladies and gentlemen,

The captain has informed us that due to a minor mechanical problem with this aircraft that our departure will be delayed. Our maintenance staff is working diligently to solve this problem. As your safety is our primary concern, please remain in your seat. Further information will be provided as soon as possible. Thank you for your understanding and patience!

女士们，先生们：

机长非常抱歉地通知我们，由于飞机的小故障，维修人员正在积极排除，飞机将推迟起飞。维修人员会本着严谨的工作态度尽快排除故障。完全是我们最重视的，请您在座位上休息等候，我们将随时广播通知您进一步的消息。谢谢您的谅解和支持！

3. 飞机配载平衡广播

Ladies and gentlemen,

For the balance of the aircraft, please follow the instructions of our ground staff, sit after row 16. Thank you for your cooperation!

女士们，先生们：

为了飞机起飞时的配载平衡，请您在地面工作人员的安排下在16排后就座。谢谢您的配合！

4. 中止起飞广播

Ladies and gentlemen,

As you've noticed, the captain has aborted the take-off for safety concern. We will give you more information as soon as it becomes available.

女士们，先生们：

正如我们之前的通知，由于安全原因，机长终止了起飞，请您在座位上扣好安全带。如果问题已解决，我们将及时通知您。

5. 等待摆渡车或者廊桥广播

Ladies and gentlemen,

Please remain seated while waiting for the shuttle bus/boarding bridge at Airport.

Thank you for your cooperation.

女士们，先生们：

由于机场的摆渡车/廊桥未到，请您在座位上等待，感谢您的配合。

Part IV Words and Expressions

1. instruction /ɪnˈstrʌkʃn/ n. 指示；指令；吩咐
2. minor /ˈmaɪnə(r)/ adj. 较小的；次要的；轻微的
3. mechanical /məˈkænɪkl/ adj. 机械般的；呆板的
4. maintenance /ˈmeɪntənəns/ n. 维护；保养
5. diligence /ˈdɪlɪdʒəns/ n. 勤奋，用功
6. row /rəʊ , raʊ/ n.（剧院，体育场等的）一排座位；一排，一行
7. abort /əˈbɔːt/ v.（使）流产；中止（计划等）
8. safety /ˈseɪfti/ n. 安全；平安
9. concern /kənˈsɜːn/ n. 影响；涉及；牵涉（某人或者某事）
10. primary /ˈpraɪməri/ adj. 主要的；最重要的；基本的

Part V Reading Skill

朗读节奏划分技巧

Reading Rhythm Division Skills

朗读时，声带所产生的音量是很小的，占音量的5%左右，其他95%左右的音量，需要通过共鸣腔放大得来。节奏是指朗读过程中由声音抑扬顿挫、轻重缓急而形成的回环往复的形式。常见的节奏类型大体有：

（1）轻快型：这种节奏语速较快，多扬少抑，多轻少重，声轻不着力，词语密度大，有时有跳越感，多用来描绘欢快、诙谐的情志。

（2）沉稳型：这种节奏语势沉缓，多抑少扬，多重少轻，音强而着力，词语密度疏，常用来表现庄重、肃穆的气氛和悲痛、抑郁的情感。

（3）舒缓型：这种节奏语速较缓，语势较平稳，声音轻柔而不着力，常常用来描绘幽静的场面和美丽的景色，也可以表现舒展的情怀。

（4）强疾型：这种节奏语速较快，多扬少抑，声音强劲而有力，常用来表现紧张急迫的情形和抒发激越的情怀。

Part VI Practical Practice

1. Match the expressions in Column A with their Chinese equivalents in Column B.

Column A   Column B
(1) beverage   a. 指令
(2) instruction   b. 主要的
(3) primary   c. 饮料
(4) row   d. 保养；维护
(5) maintenance   e. 一排

2. Translate the following sentences into English.

（1）由于航路交通管制，目前我们暂时无法确定起飞时间。

（2）请大家在座位上休息等候，如果有进一步的消息，我们会尽快通知您。

3. Translate the following sentences into Chinese.

(1) We will be serving food and beverages while we are waiting for departure.

(2) The captain has informed us that due to a minor mechanical problem with this aircraft that our departure will be delayed.

4. Practice oral English.

(1) Ladies and gentlemen,

May I have your attention please?

We regret to inform you that due to mechanical problem we will have to change to another aircraft. Please take all your belongings when you disembark and follow our ground staff to the new aircraft.

We apologize for any inconvenience. Your understanding and cooperation will be very much appreciated.

(2) Ladies and gentlemen,

The parking area has not been cleared for our aircraft arrival and we have been requested by local Air Traffic Control to hold here. Our ground staff is working on a solution at this time. Please remain in your seat.

Thank you for your cooperation!

(3) Ladies and gentlemen,

We must keep the balance for the aircraft. Please take your seat according to your seat.

Thank you.

Task 26
On Stopover

Too much liberty spills all.
自由放任，一事无成。

Learning Objectives
Knowledge Objectives
1. To know how to make an announcement on stopover
2. To learn some useful expressions on stopover
Skill Objectives
1. To be able to master the key words and expressions on stopover
2. To be able to know to cultivate the charm of voice
Quality Objectives
1. To develop the sense of responsibility
2. To be knowledgeable and professional

Part I Lead-in

Question:

Stopover means landing at a place for a second time or loading goods on the way. When stopping, how many kinds of arrangements for passengers on board?

Task 26   On Stopover

Part II   Background Information

经停的时候，机上旅客有 2 种安排：一种是下飞机，在候机室等候；另一种是不用下飞机。根据飞行要求和地勤安排，空中乘务员会协助旅客处理。经停有国内经停国内航班、国内经停国际航班两种类型。

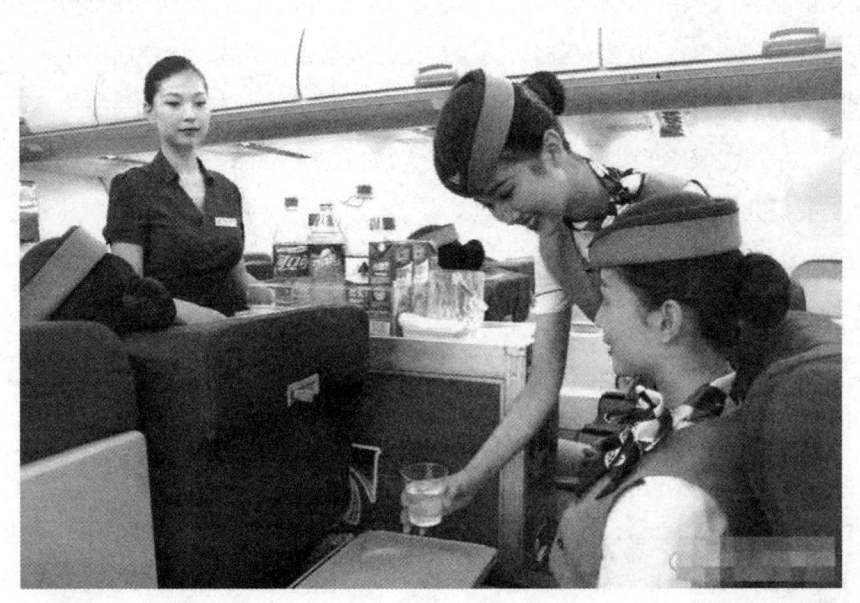

Part III   Let's Read

1. 国内经停国内航班播音

Ladies and gentlemen:

We have just landed at Ji Nan Yao Qiang Airport. The outside temperature is 10 degrees Celsius, 50 degrees Fahrenheit. Please remain seated until our aircraft stops completely. Please be cautious when retrieving items from the overhead bin. Passengers leaving the aircraft at this airport, please take all your belongings when you disembark. Your checked baggage may be claimed in the baggage claim area.

Those passengers continuing to Shen Zhen, when you disembark, please take your ticket or boarding pass with you, and obtain a transit card from the ground staff, then proceed to the waiting hall. We will be here for about 40 minutes. Your hand baggage may be left on board but take your valuables with you.

133

Thank you for flying with us. Have a pleasant day!

女士们，先生们：

我们的飞机已经降落在本次航班的中途站济南遥墙机场，外面的温度是10摄氏度、50华氏度。

飞机还需要滑行一段时间，请保持安全带扣好。等飞机安全停稳后，请您小心开启行李架。

到达济南的旅客，请带好您的全部手提物品下飞机，您的交运行李请在到达厅领取。

继续前往深圳的旅客，当您下机时，请带好您的机票或登机牌，向地面工作人员领取过站登机牌，到候机厅休息等候。我们的飞机将在这里停留40分钟左右，您的手提物品可以放在飞机上，但贵重物品请您随身携带。

感谢您与我们共同度过这段美好的行程！

2. 国内经停国际航班播音

Ladies and gentlemen:

We have just landed at Da Lian Zhou Shuizi International Airport. The outside temperature is 10 degrees Celsius, 50 degrees Fahrenheit.

Please remain seated until our aircraft stops completely. Please be cautious when retrieving items from the overhead bin. passengers leaving the aircraft at this airport, please take all your belongings when you disembark. Your checked baggage may be claimed in the baggage claim area. Passengers leaving the aircraft at this airport, please take your passport and all your belongings to complete the entry formalities in the terminal. Your checked baggage may be claimed in the baggage claim area.

Passengers continuing to Hiroshima, attention please! The aircraft will stay here for about one hour. When you disembark, please get your transit card from the ground staff, and complete your exit formalities and quarantine here.

According to Customs Regulations of the People's Republic of China, please take all carry-on items with you when you go through Customs. Any baggage left on board will be handed by the Customs. Formalities for checked baggage will be complete at the customs counter.

Thank you for flying with us. Have a pleasant day!

女士们，先生们：

我们的飞机已经降落在本次航班的中途站——大连周水子国际机场，外面的温度是10摄氏度、50华氏度。

飞机还需要滑行一段时间，请保持安全带扣好。等飞机安全停稳后，请您小心开启行李架。

到达大连的旅客，请带好您的全部手提物品下飞机，您的交运行李请在到达厅领取。

继续前往广岛的旅客请注意：飞机在这里大约停留 1 小时左右。当您下机时，请向地面工作人员领取过站登机牌。请您在本站办理出境及检疫手续。根据中华人民共和国海关规定，请将您的全部手提物品带下飞机，接受海关检查。对遗留在飞机上的、未经海关检查的行李物品，将由海关人员处理。交运行李的海关手续将在海关柜台办理。

Part IV Words and Expressions

1. transit /ˈtrænzɪt/ *n.* 运输，运送；经过
2. passport /ˈpɑːspɔːt/ *n.* 护照
3. formality /fɔːˈmæləti/ *n.* 礼节；拘谨；正式手续
   exit formalities 出境手续
4. quarantine /ˈkwɒrəntiːn/ *n.*（为防传染的）隔离期；检疫
5. belongings /bɪˈlɒŋɪŋz/ *n.* 随身携带行李
6. retrieve /rɪˈtriːv/ *v.* 找回；收回
7. disembark /ˌdɪsɪmˈbɑːk/ *v.* 登陆；下（车、船、飞机等）
8. claim /kleɪm/ *v.* 提出要求；声称

Part V Reading Skill

如何培养声音的魅力
How to Cultivate the Charm of Voice

男士的明朗、低沉、愉快的语调最具有吸引力，但应注意激昂时的情绪控制及对方的反应。而女士则以柔和、愉快、明朗的语调为宜。说话时要注意速度的快慢，咬字要清晰，发音要准确，段落要分清，声音的大小要适中、适度。如果你想在播音中给人以明朗、畅快的感觉，就应该注意语言要清晰，语音、频率要稍高一些，转折音要柔和。这样，注重声音的大小，语调的高低，一定能为你的声音增色不少。练习呼吸时要有一定的呼吸储量，要口鼻共同呼吸，气沉丹田，呼吸自如。播音是要抒发一种情怀、一种心情，以引起听众的共鸣，所以应在正确理解、深刻把握稿件的基础上，全身心投入感情。

Part VI   Practical Practice

1. Match the expressions in Column A with their Chinese equivalents in Column B.

Column A   Column B

(1) boarding pass   a. 登机牌

(2) passport   b. 过境证

(3) transit card   c. 出境手续

(4) exit formalities   d. 检疫

(5) quarantine   e. 护照

2. Translate the following sentences into English.

（1）遗留在飞机上的、未经海关检查的行李物品，将由海关人员处理。

（2）交运行李的海关手续将在海关柜台办理。

3. Translate the following sentences into Chinese.

(1) Your hand baggage may be left on board but take your valuables with you.

(2) Passengers leaving the aircraft at this airport, please take your passport and all your belongings to complete the entry formalities in the terminal.

4. Practice oral English.

(1) Ladies and gentlemen,

We are sorry to inform you that we are heading direct to _____ Airport due to unfavorable weather conditions at _____ Airport (airport has been closed). We expect to land at _____ Airport at about _____ a.m./ p.m. We apologize for the inconvenience.

Thank you for your cooperation!

(2) Attention please!

Passengers continuing to other cities with_____ Airlines should take all your carry-on luggage and disembark. Please contact our ground staff for transfer procedures.

Task 27

Air Condition Problem

Too much knowledge makes the head bald.
学问太多催人老。

Learning Objectives
Knowledge Objectives 1. To know how to make an announcement about air condition problem 2. To learn some useful expressions about air condition problem **Skill Objectives** 1. To be able to master the key words and expressions 2. To be able to know the reading skill-linking **Quality Objectives** 1. To develop the sense of responsibility 2. To be knowledgeable and professional

Part I Lead-in

Question:

Air Condition Problem happens occasionally on the flight. If it happens, what shall we do meantime?

Task 27 Air Condition Problem

Part II Background Information

飞机空调在飞机停靠登机廊桥到飞机离开廊桥这段时间，为乘客和机组人员提供舒适的机舱环境。

Part III Let's Read

空调制冷效果不佳的安抚广播

1. Ladies and gentlemen,

As the air conditioning system of this aircraft does not work well on the ground, you may feel a little hot at the moment. We are sorry for this inconvenience. After take-off, the cabin temperature will get down. Your understanding will be much appreciated.

女士们，先生们：

由于本架飞机的空调系统在地面停留期间制冷效果不太理想，造成目前机舱温度较高，对给您带来的不适，我们深表歉意。这种情况在飞机起飞后会很快缓解。谢谢！

2. Ladies and gentlemen,

We are now waiting for the flight departure. You may feel a little bit hot now due to the air conditioning system doesn't work well before take-off. We regret for this inconvenience at the moment. You may feel better after take-off. Thank you!

女士们，先生们：

我们现在正在等待起飞，由于本架飞机在地面停留期间的空调制冷效果不够理想，造成目前客舱温度偏高，给您带来不适，我们深表歉意，这种情况在飞机起飞后会很快缓解。谢谢！

3. Ladies and gentlemen,

Our flight is waiting for take-off because the engine has not been started, the air-conditioner cooling/heating system may not be effective during this period. We apologize for any discomfort it may cause due to the high/cold temperature.

This situation will be improved after take-off.

女士们，先生们：

我们的航班正在等待起飞，因为发动机尚未启动，在此期间空调冷却/加热系统可能无效。对于由于高温/低温而可能造成的任何不适，我们深表歉意。

这种情况在起飞后会得到改善。

Part IV　Words and Expressions

1. air conditioning system　空调系统
2. temperature /ˈtemprətʃə(r)/ n. 温度；体温；氛围
3. inconvenience /ˌɪnkənˈviːniəns/ n. 不方便；麻烦
4. effective /ɪˈfektɪv/ adj. 有效的
5. period /ˈpɪəriəd/ n. 一段时间；阶段
6. discomfort /dɪsˈkʌmfət/ n. 不舒适，不舒服

Part V　Reading Skill

连读

Linking

连读是在英语交流中，使用较快语速时，相邻的两词所发生的类似单词拼读的语音现象。两词连读一般应具备以下条件：相邻两词在意义上必须密切相关，同属一个意群。

连读构成的音节一般不重读，只需顺其自然地一带而过，不可读得太重。连读主要出现在意义联系较紧的词，如冠词与名词、数词与名词、动词与副词、连接词与代名词之间。

语意自然停顿的地方，即有逗号、句号等标点符号的地方，不用连读。英语中常见的连读

Task 27 Air Condition Problem

现象主要有以下 4 种：

（1）"辅音+元音"型连读。在同一个意群里，如果相邻两词中的前一个词是以辅音结尾的，后一个词是以元音开头的，这就要将辅音与元音拼起来连读。

I'm~an~English boy.

It~is~an~old book.

Let me have~a look~at~it.

Ms Black worked in~an~office last~yesterday.

I called~you half~an~hour~ago.

（2）"r/re+元音"型连读。

如果前一个词是以-r 或者-re 结尾的，后一个词是以元音开头的，这时的 r 或 re 不但要发/r/，而且还要与后面的元音拼起来连读。

They're my father~and mother.

I looked for~it here~and there.

There~is a football under~it.

There~are some books on the desk.

Here~is a letter for you.

Here~are four~eggs.

But where~is my cup?

Where~are your brother~and sister?

然而，如果一个音节的前后都有字母 r，即使后面的词以元音开头，也不能连读。

The black clouds are coming nearer and nearer.（nearer 与 and 不可连读。）

（3）"辅音+半元音"型连读。

英语语音中的/j/和/w/是半元音，如果前一个词是以辅音结尾的，后一个词是以半元音的，特别是/j/开头，此时也要连读。

Thank~you.

Nice to meet~you.

Did~you get there late~again?

Would~you like~a cup~of tea?

Could~you help me, please?

"音的同化"——常把/d/+/j/读成/dV/, did you 听成了/dIdVu/, would you 听成了/wudVu/, could you 听成了/kudVu/。

（4）"元音+元音"型连读。

如果前一个词以元音结尾，后一个词以元音开头，这两个音往往也要自然而不间断地连读到一起。

I~am Chinese.

He~is very friendly to me.

She wants to study~English.

How~and why did you come here?

She can't carry~it.

It'll take you three~hours to walk there.

The question is too~easy for him to answer.

Part VI Practical Practice

1. Match the expressions in Column A with their Chinese equivalents in Column B.

Column A   Column B

(1) temperature   a. 温度

(2) air conditioning system   b. 不便

(3) inconvenience   c. 改善

(4) engine   d. 空调系统

(5) improve   e. 发动机

2. Translate the following sentences into English.

（1）由于本架飞机起飞前空调系统不能正常工作，您可能会感觉到一些闷热。

（2）对给您带来的不适，我们深表歉意。

3. Translate the following sentences into Chinese.

(1) As the air conditioning system of this aircraft does not work well on the ground, you may feel a little hot at the moment.

(2) We apologize for any discomfort it may cause due to the high temperature.

4. Practice oral English.

(1) Ladies and gentlemen,

This is your chief purser speaking. We are awfully sorry for the uncomfortable feeling caused by the cooling system of our flight. We thank you for your kind understanding, patience and cooperation.

(2) Ladies and gentlemen,

With the excellent work of our crew and maintenance people, the air-condition system is working properly now. You will feel better soon. We thank you for your understanding and cooperation. Now please be seated and ready for a safe take-off.

Thank you!

(3) Ladies and gentlemen,

It is very slippery outside because of rain. Please watch your steps as you disembark.

Thank you!

Task 28
Safety Check Broadcast before Landing

Better to ask the way than go astray.
问路总比迷路好。

Learning Objectives
Knowledge Objectives 1. To know how to make an announcement safety check broadcast before landing 2. To learn some useful expressions about safety check broadcast before landing **Skill Objectives** 1. To be able to conduct a safety check broadcast 2. To be able to know to learn about the sentence stress **Quality Objectives** 1. To develop the sense of responsibility 2. To be knowledgeable and professional

Part I Lead-in

Question:

In order to make sure 100% safe, the crew members should check whether every individual is secured, so safety check before landing is indispensable. Do you know what kinds of safety checks are before landing?

Task 28 Safety Check Broadcast before Landing

Part II Background Information

为了确保旅客百分百安全，机组人员在飞机落地之前还要进行一次确认安全的检查，这一环节是必不可少的。

Part III Let's Read

Ladies and gentlemen,

We will be landing shortly. Please make sure that your seat belts are securely fastened. Seat backs and tray tables should be returned to the upright position. If you are sitting beside a window, please help us by putting up the sunshades. All personal computers and electronic devices should be turned off. And please make sure that your carry-on items are securely stowed. And for your safety, we kindly remind you that during the landing and taxiing, please do not open the overhead bin. We will be dimming the cabin lights for landing.

Thank you!

女士们，先生们：

飞机即将着陆，为了您的安全，请再次确认安全带是否已经扣好，收起小桌板，将座椅靠背调整到正常位置。靠窗边的旅客请协助将遮光板打开。所有个人电脑及电子设备必须处于关闭状态。请您确认您的手提物品是否已妥善安放。同时我们还要提醒您，在飞机着陆及滑行期间，请不要开启行李架提拿行李物品。稍后，我们将调暗客舱灯光。

谢谢！

Part IV　Words and Expressions

1. secure /sɪˈkjʊə(r)/ *adj.* 安全的；稳妥的
2. device /dɪˈvaɪs/ *n.* 装置；仪器；器具；设备
   a water-saving device　节水装置
   electronic devices　电子装备
3. carry-on　（可随身携带上飞机的）小包；小行李箱
   carry-on baggage　随身携带的行李
4. dim /dɪm/ *v.*（使）（灯光）变昏暗；（使）变暗淡
5. stow /stəʊ/ *v.* 保存；妥善放置
6. seat backs　座椅靠背
   cabin lights　客舱灯光
   tray tables　小桌板

Part V　Reading Skill

语句重音

Sentence Stress

语句重音是指根据不同的交际需要而对句子的某个或者某些词加以强调。重音的特点是：发音用力较大，音量较高，时间较长。

重音分为：表意重音、逻辑重音及情感重音。

（1）表意重音。表意重音是指讲话人在没有受个人情感影响或没有特意将句中的某一信息加以强调的情况下，对句中所有实词一视同仁地加以强调。实词包括名词、动词、形容词、副词、数词、指示代词、疑问代词等；虚词包括介词、冠词、助动词、连词、人称代词等。例如，

a. In general, we emphasize a word as we stress a syllable by giving it more force, longer duration, and higher pitch.

b. I believe the course I have followed with China is the one that's best for America, disagreeing where we have serious disagreements, pursuing our common interests where I thought it was in the interest of the United States. (Bill Clinton)

（2）逻辑重音。逻辑重音又叫对比重音，指讲话人有意将句中的某个成分（一般只有 1 个，但也有 2 个的情况）与上下文当中的另一个成分相对比而给予的特殊强调。此时，句中本来该重读的实词被读得快而弱，本来该弱读的虚词被减弱到几乎听不出来的程度。

（3）情感重音。情感重音是指说话人在处于极为激动的情况下，对某个能表达其情感的词或词组给予超常规的强调。例如，We Chinese people are unconquerable.

Part VI   Practical Practice

1. Match the expressions in Column A with their Chinese equivalents in Column B.

Column A   Column B
(1) securely   a. 设备
(2) device   b. 电子的
(3) electronic   c. 安全地
(4) stow   d. 保存
(5) tray tables   e. 小桌板

2. Translate the following sentences into English.

（1）请确认安全带是否已经扣好。

（2）请确认您的手提物品是否已妥善安放。

3. Translate the following sentences into Chinese.

(1) If you are sitting beside a window, please help us by putting up the sunshades.

(2) All personal computers and electronic devices should be turned off.

4. Practice oral English.

Ladies and gentlemen,

We are beginning our final descent. Please fasten your seatbelts, return your seat back to the upright position and stow your tray table, and return your footrest to its initial position. Please help us by opening the sunshades. All laptop computers and electronic devices should be turned off at this time. We kindly remind you that during landing and taxiing, please keep your seatbelts fastened and do not open the overhead compartment. We will be dimming the cabin lights for landing.

Thank you!

Task 29
Landing on the Ground

Health is better than wealth.
健康胜于财富。

微课抢先看

Learning Objectives
Knowledge Objectives
1. To know how to make an announcement landing on the ground
2. To learn some useful expressions about landing on the ground
Skill Objectives
1. To be able to master the words and expressions about landing on the ground
2. To be able to know weak forms
Quality Objectives
1. To develop the sense of responsibility
2. To be knowledgeable and professional

Part I Lead-in

Question:

What can be said when the flight is landing on the ground?

Part II Background Information

通常从飞机落地到出机场需要 15~60 分钟，若是小型机场不等候行李，至少需要 15 分钟左右；若是大型机场不等候行李，至少需要 30 分钟左右。飞机落地后，需要等待一段时间，因为机场的各个区域都需要收到相应的指令之后才能够具体行动，除此之外，乘客还要拿自己托运的行李，若排队等候行李需再额外增加 30 分钟左右。

Part III Let's Read

Ladies and gentlemen,

We have just landed at Beijing Capital International Airport. It is 3:25 p.m. of November 20th by the local time. The temperature outside is 15 degrees Celsius, 59 degrees Fahrenheit. Please remain seated until our aircraft stops completely. Please be cautious when retrieving items from the overhead bin. When you disembark, please take all your belongings. Your checked baggage may be claimed in the arrival hall. Passengers with connecting flights, please go to the transfer counter in the terminal. Once again, we apologize for the delay of our flight. We thank you for your cooperation and understanding. Thank you for choosing China Southern Airlines. It has been a pleasure looking after you and we hope to see you again. Thank you!

女士们，先生们：

欢迎您来到北京首都国际机场！当地时间是 11 月 20 日下午 3 点 25 分，现在机舱外面的温度是 15 摄氏度、59 华氏度。飞机还需要滑行一段时间，请保持安全带扣好。等飞机完全停稳后，请您小心开启行李架。请您带好全部手提物品，您的交运行李请在到达厅领取。需从本站转乘飞机去其他地方的旅客，请到候机厅中转柜台办理。我们再次感谢您在航班延误时对我们工作的理解与配合。南方航空，伴您一路春风！感谢您选择中国南方航空公司航班。我们期待再次与您相会，谢谢！

Part IV　Words and Expressions

1. retrieve /rɪˈtriːv/ v. 取回；索回
2. cautious /ˈkɔːʃəs/ adj. 小心的；谨慎的
3. disembark /ˌdɪsɪmˈbɑːk/ v. 下（车、船、飞机等）
4. checked baggage　所托运的行李
5. claim /kleɪm/ v. 索取，索要（有权拥有的东西）
6. formality /fɔːˈmæləti/ n. 正式手续

    exit formalities　出境手续
7. bin /bɪn/ n. 垃圾桶；箱子

    overhead bin　行李架
8. transfer /trænsˈfɜː(r)/, ˈtrænsfɜː(r)/ v. 转移；调动；转让

    transfer counter　中转柜台
9. terminal /ˈtɜːmɪnl/ n. 航空站；终点站；集散地

    in the terminal　在候机厅
10. arrival /əˈraɪvl/ n. 到达；到达者/物

    arrival hall　到达厅

Part V　Reading Skill

Weak Forms
弱读

弱读的规定如下：实词（动词、名词、形容词、副词）重读，而虚词（介词、代词、冠词、不定式符号）弱读。弱读的规则一般是：元音音节弱化成 /ə/ 或 /i/。例如，下几个单词：for, as, at, of, the, to, than, and, or, his, a, an, but, been, her, we, be, shall, was, them。

又如，for/fɔ:/，弱读为/fə/；as /æz/弱读为/əz/；do/du:/→/du/→/d/，of/v/→/v/→/v/，them/m/→/m/→/m/；we/wi:/→/wi/等。弱读音节中最常见的音是中元音/ʌ/被读为/ə/。some/sʌm/弱读为/səm/；does /dʌz/弱读为/dəz/；but /bʌt/弱读为/bət/。

Part VI Practical Practice

1. Match the expressions in Column A with their Chinese equivalents in Column B.

Column A   Column B

(1) retrieve   a. 谨慎的

(2) cautious   b. 索取、索要

(3) disembark   c. 下（车、船、飞机等）

(4) formality   d. 正式手续

(5) claim   e. 取回

2. Translate the following sentences into English.

（1）您的交运行李请在到达厅领取。

（2）下机时，请携带所有随身物品。

3. Translate the following sentences into Chinese.

(1) Please be cautious when retrieving items from the overhead bin.

(2) For passengers bound for Guangzhou, please prepare your passport and all your belongings to the terminal for exit formalities.

4. Practice oral English.

(1) Ladies and gentlemen,

Our airplane has arrived assigned position. Before leaving, please check to take all our carry-on

Task 29 Landing on the Ground

baggage.

Thank you!

(2) Ladies and gentlemen,

We have arrived in Xi'an, the distance between Xi'an Xianyang International Airport and downtown is 47 kilometers. It is Beijing Time 15:30. The outside temperature is 28 degrees Celsius.

We are taxiing now, for your safety, please turned off your mobile phone. In case of disturb communicate between cockpit and control tower, please do not open the overhead locker. When the airplane has come to a complete stop, we will brighten the cabin. Please open the overhead locker carefully, and then you can get ready for disembarkation.

Thank you for flying with _____ Airlines and see you next time!

Task 30
Returning to the Departure Airport

微课抢先看

All is not gold that glitters.
闪光的未必都是金子。

Learning Objectives
Knowledge Objectives
1. To know how to make an announcement returning to the departure airport
2. To learn some useful expressions about returning to the departure airport
Skill Objectives
1. To be able to conduct an announcement by using the words and expressions
2. To be able to know how to control the breath with emotion
Quality Objectives
1. To develop the sense of responsibility
2. To be knowledgeable and professional

Part I Lead-in

Question:

Can you tell us what will the captain do if the air route is not suitable for flying or if there are some mechanic problems or the destination airport is closed down?

Task 30 Returning to the Departure Airport

Part II Background Information

返航就是返回原地的航程，船舶、飞机等驶回或飞回出发的地方。

Part III Let's Read

Ladies and gentlemen,

Due to bad weather on the route, the captain has decided to return to the departure airport. We expect to land there at 2:20. We will keep you updated with any information as we receive it. We apologize for any inconvenience. We sincerely appreciate your understanding.

女士们，先生们：

我们刚刚接到机长的通知，由于航路天气不符合飞行标准，我们现在必须返回机场，飞机预计在2点20分到达。对于由此给您带来的诸多不便，请予以谅解。返航后的有关事宜，我们会随时通知您。谢谢！

Part IV   Words and Expressions

1. decide /dɪˈsaɪd/ v. 对……做出抉择；决定；选定
2. return /rɪˈtɜːn/ v. 返回；回来；回去
3. departure /dɪˈpɑːtʃə(r)/ n. 离开；启程；动身；出发
   the departure lounge/time/gate 候机室/起飞时间/登机口
   arrivals and departures 到站和离站班次
   the departures board 离站时刻牌
4. update /ˌʌpˈdeɪt/ n. 最新消息；快讯；速递
   a weather update 最新天气报告
5. runway /ˈrʌnweɪ/ n.（飞机场的）跑道
6. remain /rɪˈmeɪn/ v. 仍然是；保持不变；持续
7. complete /kəmˈpliːt/ adj. 完全的；彻底的

Part V   Reading Skill

如何掌控气息，做到"以情运气"？
How to Control the Breath with Emotion?

播音主持"以情运气"。播音中强调以情运气，气随情动。就是说对于作品的思想内容理解认识准确了，还要使思想感情随之运动起来，只有真正地动起来了，才可能气随情动，才能动得自如。播音中如果总是用冷眼旁观的态度对待稿件，无动于衷，即使嗓音条件再好、呼吸再通畅、基本功再扎实，播出来的东西也是平平淡淡、毫无味道。因此，调动思想感情的运动至关重要，只有思想感情动起来了，有了强烈的播讲愿望，呼吸才能自如地变化，语言也会富有色彩。语调生动，轻重适宜。根据需要，分出轻重缓急，分清抑扬顿挫，才能表达出文章的思想感情。

Part VI   Practical Practice

1. Match the expressions in Column A with their Chinese equivalents in Column B.

Column A   Column B
(1) decide   a. 离开

Task 30 Returning to the Departure Airport

(2) departure   b. 决定

(3) update   c. 最新消息

(4) overhead bin   d. 回去

(5) return   e. 行李架

2. Translate the following sentences into English.

（1）返航后的有关事宜，我们会随时通知您。

（2）我们由衷感谢您的理解。

3. Translate the following sentences into Chinese.

(1) Due to bad weather on the route, the captain has decided to return to the departure airport.

(2) We apologize for any inconvenience.

4. Practice oral English.

(1) Ladies and gentlemen,

May I have your attention, please?

     a. Due to bad weather/fog/a strike/a runway obstruction at _____ Airport,

(_____Airport has been closed).

     b. Due to mechanical trouble

     c. Because of heavy storm ahead of us, the captain has decided to make an additional stop. We are returning to _____ Airport. Further information will be given to you after landing. We apologize for the inconvenience.

Thank you for your cooperation!

(2) Ladies and gentlemen,

The plane has arrived at its destination airport, the Fasten Seat Belt Sign will remain illuminated while the plane is taxiing. Please remain seated with your seat belt fastened, please take all your carry-on items with you when you disembark and make sure no personal belongings are left in the seat pocket in front of you. When the plane comes to a complete stop. Please be careful when opening the overhead lockers to prevent articles from falling out. Your baggage can be claimed at the arrival hall. Thank you for choosing airlines. We apologize again for the delay. We strive to provide considerate service at all times. We look forward to serving you again in the near future.

Task 31
Landing at the Destination Airport

Seeing is believing.
百闻不如一见。

微课抢先看

Learning Objectives
Knowledge Objectives
1. To know how to make an announcement landing at the destination airport
2. To learn some useful words and expressions
Skill Objectives
1. To be able to use the words and expressions
2. To be able to master reading skill about stressed
Quality Objectives
1. To develop the sense of responsibility
2. To be knowledgeable and professional

Part I Lead-in

Question:

When we heard the flight attendant broadcast before landing, we feel very relaxed and relieved.

(1) Do you still remember what the attendants remind us to do?

(2) When the flight is about to descend?

Part II Background Information

机场、空港，较正式的名称是航空站。机场的大小不同，除了跑道，通常还设有塔台、停机坪、航空客运站、维修厂等设施，并提供机场管制服务、空中交通管制等其他服务。

Part III Let's Read

Ladies and gentlemen,

We will be landing at Harbin Taiping International Airport in about 30 minutes. It is sunny in Harbin, the temperature is minus 10 degrees Celsius and 14 degrees Fahrenheit. Because of the extreme weather difference, may we suggest you dress accordingly. The captain will switch on the Fasten Seat Belt Sign soon. Would you kindly return to your seats, stow your belongings in the overhead compartments or under the seats in front of you, place your tray tables, footrests and seat-backs upright, check your seat-belts are securely fastened. All electronic devices must be switched off at this time. The lavatories and entertainment system will be closed in 5 minutes, the cabin crew will be coming around to collect your blankets and headsets, and we would appreciate if you would have them ready. The plane is about to descend, and according to the requirements of the

Task 31 Landing at the Destination Airport

Chinese civil aviation regulations, we will stop all the cabin services, and the flight attendant will carry out the cabin safety inspection at a later time. At the same time, we would also like to remind you that please do not rise to open the overhead bin to pick up your luggage until the plane stops completely. Cabin pressure changes during descending, and if you feel ear pain, you can relieve it by swallowing.

Thank you!

女士们，先生们：

我们的飞机将在30分钟后到达哈尔滨太平国际机场。目前哈尔滨天气晴朗，地面温度是零下10摄氏度、14华氏度。请您及时整理随身物品，由于两地温差较大，建议您增减衣物。安全带信号灯即将亮起，洗手间和娱乐系统大约在5分钟后关闭，请将您不需要使用的毛毯和耳机交还给客舱乘务员。飞机即将开始下降高度，根据中国民航法规的要求，我们将停止一切客舱服务工作，稍后乘务员将进行客舱安全检查，为了您的安全，请您系好安全带，收起小桌板，调直座椅靠背，将脚踏板放到正常位置。打开遮光板，乘务员将统一调亮客舱舱窗，请保持飞机舱窗在明亮状态。请关闭所有电子设备，下降及着陆期间请您将随身携带的小包放在前排座椅下方或行李架内。同时我们还要提醒您，在飞机完全停稳之前，请不要起身或开启行李架提拿行李物品。下降期间，客舱压力会发生变化，如果您感觉耳痛，可以通过吞咽动作来缓解。

谢谢！

Part IV Words and Expressions

1. descend /dɪˈsend/ v. 下来；下去；下降
2. compartment /kəmˈpɑːtmənt/ n.（飞机）隔间；分隔间；隔层
3. entertainment /ˌentəˈteɪnmənt/ n. 娱乐；文娱节目；表演会；娱乐活动
   live entertainment 现场表演节目
4. remind /rɪˈmaɪnd/ v. 提醒；使想起
5. relieve /rɪˈliːv/ v. 解除；减轻；缓和（不快或痛苦）
   to relieve anxiety/guilt/stress 消除焦虑/内疚；缓解压力
   to relieve the symptoms of a cold 减轻感冒的症状
6. swallow /ˈswɒləʊ/ v. 吞下；咽下

Part V　Reading Skill

重读音节

Stressed

音节是一个最小由元音组成的声音单位，但有可选的开始和结束辅音。音节通常承载着其他语音特征，如重音、音调和音高。简单来说，一个单词的音标中有几个元音就有几个音节。首先，一般来说，单音节词几乎都按重读音节对待。单音节词多数是重读音节，标记读音时不需要使用重读符号。例如，

bag /bæg/　　　　　book /buk/　　　　　club /klʌb/

bird /bɜːd/　　　　　snail /sneɪl/　　　　　fish /fɪʃ/

pitch /pɪtʃ/　　　　　fridge /frɪdʒ/　　　　school /skuːl/

任何双音节或多音节单词的音标中，有重读音节和非重读音节，哪一个音节重读，该音节的左上方或该音节的元音上方标有这样一个重读符号"'"。

worker /ˈwəːkə/（工人）；

actor /ˈæktə/（演员）；

until /ənˈtil/（直到……）；

repeat /riˈpiːt/（重复）。

Part VI　Practical Practice

1. Match the expressions in Column A with their Chinese equivalents in Column B.

　　Column A　　　　　　　　Column B

　(1) Centigrade　　　　　　a. 摄氏度

　(2) belongings　　　　　　b. 关掉

　(3) inspection　　　　　　c. 随身物品

　(4) remind　　　　　　　　d. 检查

　(5) switch off　　　　　　e. 提醒

2. Translate the following sentences into English.

（1）由于两地温差较大，建议您增减衣物。

Task 31 Landing at the Destination Airport

（2）洗手间和娱乐系统大约在 5 分钟后关闭。

3. Translate the following sentences into Chinese.

(1) At the same time, we would also like to remind you that please do not rise to open the overhead bin to pick up your luggage until the plane stops completely.

(2) Cabin pressure changes during descending, and if you feel ear pain, you can relieve it by swallowing.

4. Practice oral English.

(1) Ladies and gentlemen,

We have arrived in _____, the distance between _____ Airport and downtown is _____ kilometers. It is Beijing Time _____. The outside temperature is _____ degrees Celsius.

We are taxiing now, for your safety, please turned off your mobile phone. In case of disturb communicate between cockpit and control tower, please do not open the overhead locker. When the airplane has come to a complete stop, we will brighten the cabin. Please open the overhead locker carefully, and then you can get ready for disembarkation.

Thank you for flying with _____ Airlines and see you next time!

(2) Ladies and gentlemen,

Our airplane has arrived assigned position. Before leaving, please check to take all our carry-on baggage.

Thank you!

Task 32

Seeing off

He that respects not is not respected.

欲受人敬，要先敬人。

微课抢先看

Learning Objectives
Knowledge Objectives
1. To know how to make an announcement seeing off
2. To learn some useful words and expressions about seeing off
Skill Objectives
1. To be able to read fluently by using the key words and expressions
2. To be able to know regulations of the past form of the verbs
Quality Objectives
1. To develop the sense of responsibility
2. To be knowledgeable and professional

Part I Lead-in

Question:

When a flight lands on the ground, what cautions should be mentioned by flight attendants besides the cozy greetings during seeing off the passengers.

Task 32　Seeing off

Part II　Background Information

乘务员站在机舱门口和客舱送别乘客，是代表航空公司、乘务组对乘坐本次航班的全体乘客表示礼仪上的道别。通过乘务员标准的站姿、耐心的引导、和蔼的目光、甜美的微笑、亲切的称呼、真诚的问候、谦诚的鞠躬，可以综合体现出乘务员的素质和修养，体现出航空公司对每位乘客的尊重与热情。

Part III　Let's Read

Ladies and gentlemen,

Welcome to Xi'an. We will be arriving at Terminal 1 at Xian Yang International Airport.

Please remain seated and keep your mobile phones switched off. Please do not open the overhead locker until the aircraft has come to a complete stop. Checked-in baggage may be claimed at the baggage carousel. If you are making a connection, please take all of your carry-on items and disembark. The ground staff will provide connecting information for you. For those passengers who are continuing to other cities abroad or domestic, Please contact our ground staff. We are pleased to welcome you to our comfortable premium transfer lounge in Departure Hall of Terminal 1 for free. Our staff there are available to offer you best service.

If you are continuing to Lan Zhou, please remain seated until we have further information for you. All that remains for me to say at this time is thank you for choosing to fly with South Airlines Company. And we look forward to seeing you again!

Thank you!

女士们，先生们：

欢迎来到西安。我们的飞机将停靠在咸阳国际机场 1 号航站楼。

请您不要站立，并保持手机关闭。等飞机完全停稳后，届时请您开启行李架。您交运的行李请到行李传送带提取。联程乘客请携带您的全部行李，下机后请听从地面工作人员的指引。转乘航班前往国内外其他城市的旅客，请联系地勤人员，T1 航站楼二楼出发厅，为您准备了高端舒适的中转休息室，免费提供中转候机服务。

继续前往兰州的旅客，请您留在座位上，我们将第一时间告知您进一步消息。感谢您选乘南方航空公司班机。南方航空公司期待与您再次同行。

谢谢！

Part IV　Words and Expressions

1. staff /stɑ:f/ *n.* 全体职工（或雇员）

    teaching staff　全体教师

    staff members　职工

    staff development/training　员工培养/培训

2. premium /ˈpri:miəm/ *adj.* 优质的；高端的

3. available /əˈveɪləb(ə)l/ *adj.* 可获得的；可购得的；可找到的

    available resources/facilities　可利用的资源/设备

4. offer /ˈɒfə(r)/ *v.* 主动提出；自愿给予

5. look forward to　（高兴地）盼望；期待

6. transfer lounge　中转休息厅

    domestic flights　国内航班

    departure hall　出发大厅

    seat pocket　座椅口袋

    connecting information　中转信息

    baggage carousel　行李传送带

arrival hall 到达厅

overhead locker 头顶行李箱

Part V Reading Skill

动词过去式的读音

the Past Form of the Verbs

动词加 ed 的读音主要有 3 种：

第一种以清辅音结尾的读 t，如 worked，asked，helped，watched，stopped

第二种以浊辅音和元音结尾的读 d，如 rained，enjoyed，studied，moved，called

第三种以 t 和 d 结尾的读 id，如 created，planted，wanted，needed

Part VI Practical Practice

1. Match the expressions in Column A with their Chinese equivalents in Column B.

Column A   Column B

(1) staff   a. 职工

(2) available   b. 自愿给予

(3) offer   c. 期待

(4) expect   d. 高端的

(5) premium   e. 可获得的

2. Translate the following sentences into English.

（1）请您不要站立，并保持手机电源关闭。

（2）您交运的行李请到机场到达厅提取。

3. Translate the following sentences into Chinese.

(1) We are pleased to welcome you to our comfortable premium transfer lounge in Departure Hall of Terminal 5 for free.

(2) All that remains for me to say at this time is thank you for choosing to fly with South Airlines Company.

4. Practice oral English.

Ladies and gentlemen,

  We have just landed at _____ Airport Terminal _____. The ground temperature is _____ degrees Celsius or _____ degrees Fahrenheit. Please remain seated with your seatbelt fastened and luggage stowed. The use of mobile phones is prohibited until the seatbelt sign is switched off. Be careful when you open the overhead compartments.

  (We apologize again for the delay due to_____.)

  Thank you for flying with _____ Airlines and see you next time!

Appendix
Words and Expressions

一、航空器（aircraft）

（一）航空器设备（aircraft equipment）

风挡 windshield/windscreen
蒙皮 skin
前部 front（fore）part
后部 rear（aft）part
内侧发动机 inboard engine or inboards
外侧发动机 outboard engine or outboards
发动机吊舱 nacelle
轮舱 wheel well
主轮 main landing wheel
前轮 nose wheel
（大）机翼（main）wing
机翼前缘 leading edge
机翼后缘 trailing edge
翼尖 wing tip
操纵面 control surface
副翼 ailerons
缝翼 slots/slats
升降舵 elevators
方向舵 rudder
漏胎 flat type
轮胎被扎破 puncture
排气道和尾锥 tail cone
天线 antenna
客舱 passenger cabin
地板 floor
顶棚（板）ceiling
机上厨房 galley
厕所 toilet
前（后）货舱 forward（after）hold
航行灯 navigation light
左（右）着陆灯 left（right）landing lamp
闪光灯 flash light
警告灯 warning light

（二）航空器系统（aircraft system）

1. 动力系统（powerplant system）

辅助动力装置 APU（auxiliary power unit）
螺旋桨 propeller
风车 windmill
外来物损伤 FOD（foreign object damage）

169

发动机失效 engine failure

发动机熄火 engine flame out

抖动 vibration

马力小 the engine is low on power

停车 engine shutdown

发动机喘振 engine surge

振动 vibration

动作筒 actuator

风扇 fan

2. 燃油系统（fuel system）

燃油箱 fuel tank

燃油泵 fuel pump

燃油油压过低警告灯 low fuel pressure warning lights

煤油 kerosene

航空煤油 aviation kerosene

升压，增压（泵）boost（pump）

放油 fuel dumping/jettison

消耗 consume

油箱 fuel tank

油量不足 short of fuel

不充足 insufficient

剩余 remain

燃油增压泵 fuel booster pump

燃油（滑油）压力低 fuel（oil）pressure low（drop）

3. 液压（滑油）系统 hydraulic（oil）system

滑油温度表 oil temperature indicator

千斤顶 jacks

密封圈 seals

活门 valve

4. 电器系统（electrical system）

发电机 generator motor

无线电设备 radio equipment

（备份）保险丝（spare）fuse

电线 wire

插头 plug

电路 circuit

跳开关 circuit breaker

电瓶（电压）battery（voltage）

调压器 voltage regulator

5. 空调系统（air-conditioning system）

释压 decompression

失密 pressure failure

冷却 cooling

加热 heating

氧气面罩 oxygen mask

流量 flow

驾驶舱加温 pilot cabin heat

6. 刹车系统（brake system）

刹车 brakes

刹车不可靠 the brakes are unreliable

刹车状况不好 braking action is poor

松刹车 brakes released

刹车 brakes set

气刹车 pneumatic braking

手刹车 manual braking

7. 应急系统（emergency system）

灭火系统 extinguisher system

防冰系统 deicing system

超温（过热）overheat

发动机灭火瓶 engine fire bottles

翼除冰 wing deicing

（三）驾驶舱（cockpit）

1. 操纵系统（control system）

飞行操纵系统 flight control system

飞行管理计算机系统（FMCS）flight management computer system

人工操纵系统 manual controls

自动驾驶操纵系统 autopilot controls

仪表着陆系统 instrument landing system

中央操纵台 center console

操纵台 control stand

控制板 control panel

杆 levers/stick/column

操纵杆 control column

操纵手柄 handle

油门 thrust levers

按钮或旋钮 knobs

开关 switch

曲柄（摇把）cranks

前轮转弯手操作盘 nose wheel steering hand wheel

机内通话 inter communication

耳机 head set

装载与配平系统 weight and balance system

2. 航空器仪表（aircraft instrument）

仪表 instrument/gauge/indicator

仪表板 instrument panel

顶部仪表板 overhead panel

主显示系统 primary display system

指示器 indicator

飞行指引仪 flight director

备份地评议 stand by gyro-horizon

发动机仪表 engine indicator

高度表 altimeter

无线电高度表 radio altimeter

空速表 airspeed indicator

刹车压力表 brake pressure gauge

超温（过热）overheat

3. 航空器动作（aircraft manoeuvre）

俯仰 pitch/tilt

横滚 roll

偏转 yaw

压坡度 bank the aircraft

抬（提）起 lift off/rotate

抬机头 pitch up the aircraft（to nose up）

推机头 pitch down the aircraft（to nose down）

大角度爬升 climb steeply

修正动作 corrective action

改平 level off

失速 stall

螺旋 spin

从失速中改出 recover from stall

急转弯 sharp turn

减慢（速度）slow down

跟踪 trail

二、气象（meteorology）

（一）云（cloud）

云底高 ceiling

少云 FEW 1~2/8, fe

疏云 SCT 3~4/8, scattered

裂开云，多云 5~7/8, broken

满天云 8/8, overcast（continuous）

在云中 in cloud

断续云中 in and out of cloud

云在增加 cloud is building up

云在消散 cloud is clearing up/dissipating

积雨云 CB（cumulonimbus）

塔状积雨云 towering cumulonimbus

（二）能见度（visibility）

晴空 sky clear

薄雾 mist

轻雾 light fog

浓雾 dense fog

吹雾，平流雾 drifting fog

雾在消散 fog is clearing up

雾越来越浓 fog is getting worse

烟 smoke

烟雾 smog

沙暴 sandstorm

（三）风（wind）

风 wind

地面风 surface wind

无风（静风）wind calm

微风 light wind

中速风 moderate wind

强风 strong wind

顺风 tailwind

顶风 headwind

侧风 crosswind

阵风 gust

风向风速仪 wind-gauge

稳定风 steady wind

风向不稳定 variable wind

风越来越大 the wind is getting stronger

风切变 wind shear

风暴 storm

（四）颠簸（turbulence）

晴空颠簸 clear air turbulence

中度颠簸 moderate turbulence

重度颠簸 severe turbulence

平稳的 smooth

上升气流 up draught

下降气流 down draught

高空急流 jet stream

（五）降水（precipitation）

小雨 light rain

大雨 heavy rain

间歇性雨 intermittent rain

连续性降水 continuous rain

偶尔下阵雨 occasional showers

零零散散的阵雨 scattered showers

毛毛雨 drizzle

雪 snow

冻雨 freezing rain

雨夹雪 sleet

飑（线）squall

飓风 hurricane

龙卷风 tornado

冰雹 hail

雷暴 thunderstorm

闪电光 flash of lightning

闪电 lightning

雹暴 hailstorm

雪暴 snowstorm

结冰 icing

(六) 温度 (temperature)

外界温度，大气温度 outside air temperature

温度在上升 the temperature is rising

温度在下降 the temperature is falling/dropping

温度稳定 the temperature is steady

(七) 跑道道面状况 (runway surface condition)

正在融化的雪 melting snow

雪水 (或半化的雪) slush

雪堆 snow drift

雪清除 snow clearance

跑道上有结冰 the runway is icy

冰块 (跑道上结的块冰) ice patches

跑道湿 the runway is wet

跑道滑 the runway is slippery

积水 pools of water/ standing water/ floodwater

刹车效应差 braking action is poor

刹车效应好 braking action is good

刹车效应中 braking action is medium

三、机场车辆 (airport vehicle)

地面车辆 ground vehicle/car

机坪车辆 ramp vehicle

引导车 follow me car

空调车 air condition car

运送乘客巴士 shuttle bus

大客车 coach

摆渡车 airport passenger bus/ferry

餐车 galley service truck

食品车 (配餐车) catering truck

拖杆 tow bar

机载客梯 air stairs/steps

地面电源车 ground power vehicle (unit)

气源车 pneumatic

救火车 fire engine (truck)

救护车 ambulance

急救车 first-aid

油车 tank car

供水车 water service truck

平台车 dolly

保安运货车 security van

牵引车 tractor

犁雪车 snow plough

吹雪车 runway snow blower

吊臂车 cherry-picker

起重机 crane

四、地面相关设备与服务 (relevant ground equipment and service)

服务设备 furnishing equipment

医疗服务 medical service

安全服务 safety services

候机楼 terminal

客/停机坪 apron/ramp

廊桥 (英) air bridge/loading bridge

登机口 passenger gate

海关 customs

输送带 conveyor

地勤 ground handling

机库 hangar

航空运货单 air waybill

登机 embark/board

轮挡 wheel chock

风挡刮水器（美）windshield wiper

风挡刮水器（英）windscreen wiper

下飞机，从飞机上卸下 disembark/unload

地面电源插座 external socket

地面电源 ground power

外部电源 external power

拔下地面（外部）电源 disconnect ground（external）power

接上地面（外部）电源 reset ground（external）power

气源 start air

供气 supply start air

拔下（接上）气源 disconnect（reset）start air unit

消防队 fire service/assistance

故障排除 trouble shooting/fixed

五、关于非正常情况和紧急情况的词汇及词组

A

abort take-off/reject/abandon 中断起飞

a flock of birds 一群鸟

adjust 调整

airborne 升空

active runway（runway in use）正在使用的跑道

air conditioning smoke 空调冒烟

anonymous call（letter）匿名电话（信）

anti-icing system inoperative 防冰系统故障

allocate 分配

aileron 副翼

auxiliary 辅助的

attack 攻击

B

backtrack 调头

belly landing（gear up landing）机腹落地

bird strike 鸟击

birds ingestion 吸鸟

bomb 炸弹

breaking action 刹车效应

braking action poor 刹车效应差

burn off 消耗

baggage loader 传送带

blast fence 气流挡板

C

cabin fire 客舱失火

caution wake turbulence 注意尾流

cabin temperature is rising 客舱温度升高

cargo fire/smoke 货舱失火/冒烟

center of gravity to the rear 重心靠后

commence 开始

converging 会聚

cockpit window broken 驾驶舱窗户出现问题

converging traffic 汇聚飞机

conflict 冲突

cough 咳

crack（使）破裂

chemicals of industrial 化学品

crane operating=hoist 吊车

D

distance 距离

destination 目的地

detect 探测

deviate from the corridor 偏出走廊

discharge extinguisher（agent）喷射灭火瓶（灭火剂）

ditching 水上迫降

dumping（jettison）放油

debris=fragments（metal strips）碎片

dense smoke 浓烟

drunk 醉酒的

dispatch 派遣

decelerating 减速

disease outbreak 疾病暴发

detonate explosive 引爆炸药

E

electric smoke or fire 电器冒烟或火警

emergency braking 应急刹车

emergency descent 紧急下降

emergency evacuation 紧急撤离

emergency gear extension not available（failure）应急放轮不成功

emergency gear extension 应急放轮

emergency landing 紧急落地

engine failure 发动机失效

engine fire 发动机失火

epidemic=pandemic 流行病

F

fire engine/fire truck 救火车

fuel leak out 漏油

flame out 熄火

fly around（go round, circumnavigate, detour, offset）绕航

forced landing 迫降

fuel level is going down 燃油液面下降

fade area 盲区

fever 发烧

fuel starvation 燃料不足

fighter 战斗机

faint 晕倒

flight strip printer 飞行进程单

G

give way to 让路

glide path 下滑道

ground air 地面气源

ground power 地面电源

gun-launched area 火箭炮空地

H

hijacker 劫持者

heart attack/disease 心脏病

hydraulic pressure is dropping rapidly 液压压力快速跌落

hydraulic system leak 液压系统泄漏

automatic direction finding system 自动指引系统

hypertension lost consciousness 高血压失

去知觉

 injury 受伤

 incursion 入侵

 illuminate 照明

J

jammed stabilizer landing 安定面卡阻着陆

L

level change on route 航路上高度改变

left or right at your convenience 左右随你

low pass 低空通场

M

military movement 军事活动

maneuver left or right 左右机动

make further checks 做进一步调查

mechanical failure 机械故障

mistake/false/incorrect 错误

mountain 山脉

make a short circuit 小航线

N

no restriction 无限

noise abatement procedure 减噪音程序

nose gear steering inoperative 前轮转弯不工作

O

opposite direction 相反方向

obstacle（obstruction）障碍物

overheat 超温

orbit 盘旋

organize 组织

obese 肥胖

P

parallel runway（taxiway）平行跑道（滑行道）

PAX baggage identification 旅客行李识别

PAX evacuation 旅客撤离

PAX stairs/steps 旅客客梯

proceeding to 飞往，前往

prohibited area 禁区

priority landing 优先落地

prohibited（forbidden）area 禁区

Q

quarantine 隔离

quarrel 争吵

R

reduce 减少

revised app. clearance 修正的进近许可

registered No. 注册号码

rest route unchanged 其余航路不变

reason unknown 原因不明

returning（coming back）返场

S

same direction 同向

short of fuel 燃油短缺

skid off（slide off）滑出

slight（moderate, severe, serious）turbulence 轻度（中度，重度）颠簸

smoke continue 烟雾继续

stall 失速

stretcher 担架

structure damage 结构损坏

swine flu 猪流感

stroke 中风

sick 病

shiver 发抖

special flight 特殊飞行

T

taxi with caution 滑行小心

thunder storm 雷雨

too close to the preceding aircraft 太接近前面飞机

try to find the cause 试图查明原因

transmitter 发射机

tail strike 擦尾

turbine blades 涡轮碎片

U

unreported vehicle 未经报告的车辆

unsure position 不明位置

unaccompanied child 无人陪伴的儿童

V

visual app 目视进近

volcanic ashes 火山灰

vortex 漩涡

W

wheel well fire 轮舱失火

wind shear 风切变

windshield 风挡

work in progress ahead 前面正在施工

wheel chair 轮椅

warning light on 警告灯亮

wrong direction 错误方向

wheelchairs=handicapped 障碍人士

六、飞行中常用的单词

A

above cloud 在云上

adjacent to 靠近

advise 建议

airborne 升空

aircraft status 状况

airway 航路

all stations 各电台

approve 同意

apron 机坪

anti-icing system 防冰系统

ask for 请求

as published at the moment 暂时根据公布

at your own discretion 由你自己决定

available 有效的，可行的

B

back on course 回到航路

backtrack 180 度调头

balance 平衡

ballast 压舱板

be held up 阻碍

behind 在后面

belong to 属于

be stuck in 卡住

between 两者之间

bird strike 鸟击

birds ingestion 吸鸟

break 断开

busy 忙

buildup 雷雨

C

cabin decompression 客舱释压

cabin altitude 客舱高度

cabin fire 客舱失火

cancel 取消

calm 镇静

cannot 不能

call sign 呼叫

change 改变

cargo conveyor belt 货物传送带

check 检查

CG moved to the rear part unbalanced 重心移动，后部不平衡

check again 再检查

circle to land 反向落地

clearance 许可

close 接近

closing from right 从右接近

commence 开始

comply with 遵守

congestion 拥挤

conflicting 冲突

cross 穿越

crew 机组

crowd 拥挤

collide 撞击

D

detailed taxi instruction 详细滑行指示

delays undetermined 延误未确定

detour buildup 绕航雷雨

displace 内移

distress 遇险

ditching 水上迫降

Don't sink 不要下沉

due to broken surface 由于道面破损

due to spacing 由于间隔

due to weight 由于重量

during push back 推机期间

E

effective 有效的

encounter moderate turbulence 遇到中度颠簸

experiencing moderate turbulence 遇到中度颠簸

emergency 紧急

emergency descent 紧急下降

emergency service 应急设施

engine failure 发动机故障

established LOC 建立航道

expedite 加速

extinguish 扑灭

extend downwind 延长三边

expect higher level 预计高度

expect 预计

estimating 预计

F

facing west 面朝前面飞机

fast turn off 快速道

flame out 熄火

flight plan route 飞行计划航路

first 第一

first convenient right 第一道口右转

follow-in front of 在前面
forced 被迫的
forced landing 迫降
freighter 货机
full call sign 全呼
further advised 进一步通知
exit 出口，离开

G

gear is not down 轮未放下
glide slope (path) 下滑道
give way to 让路
ground staff 地面工作人员

H

holding area 等待区域

I

icy patches 冰片
identify 识别
I-need 需要
immediately 立即
inoperative 不工作的
instruction 指令
intercept 切入
intersection 交叉口
initially 起始

J

jam 卡阻

L

leave frequency 脱波
leave this area 离开此区域
low pass 低空通场
lose time 消磨时间

M

maintenance 维护
make orbit right 右盘旋
maybe 可能
maneuver 机动
miss turn off 错过快速道
monitor 监督/班长
moving 移动
message 信息

N

navigation 导航
nearest/closest 最近的
not below FL130 不低于FL130
unsure of my position 我的位置不确定
north east 东北
north west 西北
nose gear 前轮

O

obstacle 障碍物
orbit 盘旋
overtake 超越

P

PAX seriously ill 旅客严重生病
parking on the apron 停在停机坪
PAX stairs/steps 旅客客梯
port engine 左发
position 位置
possible reason 可能的原因
present position 目前位置
prevent 预防
problem 问题

proceed to 前往

pull in to the left 停靠到左面

pull over to the left 停靠到左面

pull up 拉升

Q

queue up 排队

R

radial 径向线

r/w vacated 跑道脱离

rapidly 迅速

reach 到达

realize 意识

reason unknown 原因不明

recommend 劝告，推荐

reduce to minimum app. 减小到最低进近速度

regulation 规章

replacement 替换件

request priority 请求优先

response 回答

resume 恢复

reclear 重新许可

request level change en route 请求航路高度改变

rescue 营救

revised 修正了的

responsibility 责任，职责

right track 右航迹

rising 上升

rudder 方向舵

S

second 第二

short count 短数

sink rate 下沉率

skid off 滑出，偏出

slot time 离场时间

snow 雪

squawk 应答机

starboard engine 右发问题

strengthen security 加强安全

struck by lightning 遭闪电击

stuck 陷入

structure 结构

sure 确信

survivals 幸存者

suspected heart attack 疑有心脏病

T

take the second left 第二道口左转

third 第三

thunderstorm 雷雨

threshold 跑道入口处

tow bar 拖杆

track out 出航

transmitter 发射机

transmitting blind 盲发

turbulence 颠簸

U

unable 不能够

unable to comply 不能执行

undercarriage 起落架

until 直到

Appendix Words and Expressions

unknown traffic 不明飞机
urgency 紧急

V

vacate 脱离
vector 航线
verify 核实

visual check 目视检查

W

waiting 等待
why overshot 为什么复飞
work in progress 在施工

反侵权盗版声明

电子工业出版社依法对本作品享有专有出版权。任何未经权利人书面许可，复制、销售或通过信息网络传播本作品的行为；歪曲、篡改、剽窃本作品的行为，均违反《中华人民共和国著作权法》，其行为人应承担相应的民事责任和行政责任，构成犯罪的，将被依法追究刑事责任。

为了维护市场秩序，保护权利人的合法权益，我社将依法查处和打击侵权盗版的单位和个人。欢迎社会各界人士积极举报侵权盗版行为，本社将奖励举报有功人员，并保证举报人的信息不被泄露。

举报电话：（010）88254396；（010）88258888
传　　真：（010）88254397
E-mail：　dbqq@phei.com.cn
通信地址：北京市万寿路173信箱
　　　　　电子工业出版社总编办公室
邮　　编：100036